Decorative Victorian Needlework

ELIZABETH BRADLEY

DECORATIVE VICTORIAN NEEDLEWORK

PHOTOGRAPHS BY TIM HILL
AND STYLED BY ZOË HILL

CLARKSON POTTER/PUBLISHERS
NEW YORK

This book is for my husband Nick and our children Anna and Nat.

My thanks to them, to my parents
and to everyone who works at Elizabeth Bradley Designs
for their support and patience during the past year.

For the splendid photographs
which are such a vital part of this book
I would like to thank Tim Hill, Zoë Hill and Adrian Swift.

Published by Clarkson N. Potter, Inc.,
201 East 50th Street,
New York, NY 10022

Published in Great Britain in 1990 by Ebury Press,
an imprint of the Random Century Group Ltd.

CLARKSON N. POTTER,
POTTER, and Colophon
are trademarks of Clarkson N. Potter, Inc.

Editors Gillian Haslam and Emma Callery
Design The Magill Design Company
Art Editor Cherriwyn Magill
Designer Elaine Hewson
Photographer Tim Hill
Assistant Adrian Swift
Stylist Zoë Hill
Flat shots photographed by Jon Stewart
Illustrator Dennis Hawkins

Library of Congress Cataloging-in-Publication Data
Bradley, Elizabeth.
   Decorative Victorian needlework: more than 25 traditional designs
 by Elizabeth Bradley; photographs by Tim Hill.
     p. cm.
   1. Canvas embroidery—Patterns.   2. Needlework, Victorian.
I. Hill, Tim.   II. Title.
TT778.C3B69 1990
746.44'2041—dc20

ISBN 0-517-58127-2

Printed in Italy

Contents

INTRODUCTION

*E*mbroidery and woolwork are enjoying something of a revival at the present time, and inspite of their busy lives, both men and women are once more experiencing the delights of this traditional pastime. I have been doing embroidery and woolwork for over twenty years and for me its pleasures are rather like the joys of gardening – in fact, I find that many of the keenest needleworkers I know are also dedicated gardeners. Both activities offer a sense of peace and well being, and both are relaxing and yet stimulating at the same time. Designing a garden or a piece of embroidery involves the same sort of planning because, in each, colours, shadows, and shapes are arranged into patterns. The endless variety that is possible ensures that there is a continued challenge and interest: the hands are busy but the mind is free to dream and ponder. Both pastimes become quite addictive.

Like all hobbies, though, they can have their frusrating moments and irritations. Slugs, snails and frost plague gardeners while fading light, twisting wool and miscounted stitches are the bane of embroiderers. These setbacks, however, only serve to accentuate that sense of achievement that is felt when a satisfactory result is reached in the end. There is nothing to beat the pleasure that comes from surveying a well completed project; be it a dewy herbaceous border first thing on a summer's morning or a finished cushion square with all its colours working in harmony and its stitches neat and even. Having finished one piece, there is the next one to look forward to and that, needless to say, will be even better.

Embroidery is a very modest and humble art form. It is as old as any branch of the fine arts yet its finest practitioners are mostly anonymous, their only claim to fame and recognition is the excellence of the work they leave behind them. Pieces that survive from the Medieval and Tudor periods are particularly exquisite and intricate, whereas later embroideries are simpler, although they have great charm and often a strongly individual character of their own. In their unassuming way, a farmer's linen smock, a needlework carpet, a sampler or a brightly coloured rag rug are as worthy of note as any painting or piece of sculpture.

Needlework design does not need to be retrospective, although mine tends to be because my tastes and interests lie in that direction. It can be innovative and new frontiers can be broken by experimenting with fresh materials and techniques. Historic stitches can be combined in new and interesting ways and some very exciting pieces have been produced by machine stitching – the whole field is open for experimentation. Embroidery is such an adaptable and variable medium for exploration, creativity and self expression that I am sure the legacy of the twentieth century, though different, will be as rich and variable as any from the past.

Embroidery strongly reflects the tastes and social conditions in which it is worked, and this is another aspect of the subject that has always fascinated me. Over the years, I have collected and dealt in antiques of all kinds, but needleworks were always my favourite things especially samplers and examples of Victorian woolwork. They eventually became my speciality and I still collect original Berlin woolwork patterns and old needlework books.

This Paisley design (see chart on page 106) is a complex and handsome repeating pattern.

My favourite needlework period is the late eighteenth and early nineteenth centuries – it was an age of great elegance. Yet although I greatly appreciate the gracious products of the needlewomen of this time, it is the more mass-produced patterns of the mid nineteenth century that have inspired me to take up my needle and sew. The heavy romanticism and often totally unsuitable subjects of the charts amuse me. The patterns are so simple in concept and yet they work well and are capable of representing an infinite variety of subjects. They have a bold, brash charm and I love to think of women in much of Europe and parts of America busily copying them and covering their houses, husbands and children with the results of their stitching. Some women from that time were, no doubt, emancipated free thinking spirits and probably detested Berlin Woolwork. Many others, I am sure, had a lovely time embroidering their cats and wreaths of rosebuds.

The Victorians had plenty of patterns and charts

This crimson, purple and olive-green colourway of the Barley Twists and Cornflowers chart seen on page 99 is a variation which would enhance any room decorated in rich autumnal colours.

favourite subjects, field and range of colours. My taste is towards an antique and historical style rather than a contemporary approach and my designs reflect this preference. Pieces of original Berlin woolwork, patterns, prints, charts, and paintings all provide me with inspiration and are reproduced to a certain degree in my designs. Some of the charts I paint are very close to an original, some are more heavily adapted, and the rest are my own designs with reference to old material of various sorts.

The use of colour is vital in woolwork. Sometimes the wool for the design works out easily and at other times it certainly does not and the prototypes need repeated unpicking and reworking. I feel that if I have learnt anything at all from the years that I spent buying antique needlework it was to be able to differentiate between the excellent and supremely decorative and the good and merely pretty examples of embroidery. I try to give each design that I paint that charm and extra special quality that would make any dealer in the decorative arts pick it out from a collection of similar objects. Perhaps my designs are the pieces that I would have loved to discover in my travels around the antique shops and salerooms of Britain and never did.

I started producing needlework kits based on Victorian designs in October 1986 as by then good original pieces were becoming increasingly scarce and expensive. It was a way of preserving some unique original designs and encapsulating into others many of the most enchanting features of nineteenth-century work. It has been a great pleasure for me that other people have liked the patterns and I hope that they have enjoyed making up the kits.

Part of the reason why Berlin woolwork was and is so popular is that it is technically easy and yet fascinating in terms of design and colour. The pieces grow fast and the work is not too hard on the eyes as it is normally done on 10 mesh canvas. The designs in this book are best done on this size mesh also. If they are worked in cross stitch they do not need to be worked on a frame and the canvas can be tucked into a workbag and carried around to be worked on anywhere. Best of all, Victorian-style woolwork is decorative and useful as the designs and colours can be chosen to suit most houses, enhancing almost any room.

To enjoy doing woolwork is one thing, but enthusiasm does tend to wear thin if there is no purpose

to choose from and needleworkers nowadays seem to have an even greater selection available. Embroidery, particularly woolwork, is going through an especially rich and interesting phase at the moment. A wide collection of patterns and ideas are produced in a constant stream by both embroiderers and several professional designers from other fields, who have turned their attention towards needlework and are producing kits to be made up. New ground is being broken all the time both with subject matter and with the use of colour and different stitches. The general high level of interest and innovation makes it more exciting for everyone who enjoys needlework as a richer and more rewarding field of endeavour is created.

Modern needlework designers take their inspiration from all sorts of things such as the natural world, other cultures and centuries, paintings, abstract designs and geometric patterns based on shapes and shadows. Everyone has their own behind it other than a rather therapeutic pleasure. Of course, finished pieces can always be given as presents and specially designed samplers and woolwork pieces do make marvellous birthday, christening or wedding gifts. The main function of embroidery in the past however was to be useful. Embroidered garments enhanced the appearance of their wearers and added to their status and in the house, items decorated with needlework were a vital part of any well appointed room. I feel that the value of woolwork as a decorative accessory has been rather lost over recent years. Cushion squares are fun to sew but there is a limit to how many cushions will fit on to a sofa or chair. There are so many other lovely objects that can be made and then used to enrich a room.

Needlework carpets are a splendid example of an item that has once more become very fashionable, while woolwork pieces make perfect coverings for dining chairs, stools and ottomans as they are attractive, comfortable to sit on and hardwearing. Walls can be adorned with hangings, pictures or bell pulls, and windows with pelmets and needlework curtain tie-backs. The texture and colours of such woolwork lends an air of richness and luxury to a room and Victorian type designs are generally suitable for all such decorative purposes, for they are not only classic and traditional but have stood the test of time. Their colours tend to be muted rather than strident and bright, as is sometimes the case with more modern designs, and they suit today's houses which are frequently furnished with a mixture of new and antique pieces. Many period fabric designs have been revived lately and are very popular as they, too, are soft and mellow in tone. The general trend seems to be towards a rich and rather eclectic mixture of objects and in this cheerful and comfortable style of decorating, Victorian woolwork can play its part very well.

This book has given me the opportunity to provide many more patterns than I could ever hope to produce as kits. I have tried to make them as varied and decorative a collection as possible and have included patterns featuring animals and flowers alongside some more abstract and geometric designs. The geometric patterns are unusual and fun to work and are marvellous for using up all those little bits of wool left over from other projects.

Apart from the usual squares for cushions and carpets, there are borders and patterned backgrounds to add interest and extra individuality to your pieces and a range of repeating patterns should help to revolutionize the covering of chairs and stools. Alternatively, nine little patchwork patterns will help to make interesting Christmas presents for years to come. At the other end of the scale there is a section devoted to carpets which is intended to encourage everyone to start on a personal family heirloom – something which every keen needleworker must be tempted to aim for.

I very much enjoyed writing this book and painting all the charts included in it. Women today do not live lives of enforced idleness, as most of us are busy working, rearing children or enjoying a well earned retirement. In spite of having limited free time, many women and quite a few men enjoy needlework as an interesting hobby and I hope that they will have fun working from the designs. The pieces created should look individual and striking wherever they are placed in a home.

HISTORY OF VICTORIAN WOOLWORK

*B*erlin woolwork is a form of cross stitch embroidery stitched with soft, bright coloured wools on to embroidery canvas which became popular in Britain and America after 1830. It subsequently remained the principle form of embroidery throughout most of the nineteenth century and is now enjoying something of a revival. To understand why this form of embroidery superceded all others, it is necessary to look at a little of what makes the nineteenth century so distinctive and different from other centuries and periods, especially the one which preceded it.

The eighteenth century is sometimes known as the age of elegance. It was basically a rural economy with men of wealth and power owning the land. New methods of agriculture were introduced by landowners such as Jethro Tull and Lord Townsend and vast tracts of land were enclosed so that their theories could be put into practice. Elegant Georgian and Palladian houses were built in the new parks and filled with furniture designed by famous makers such as Thomas Sheraton and Robert Adams. Gardens across the country were transformed to resemble idyllic natural landscapes.

Early eighteenth-century needlework reflects these trends, especially in a form of canvas work where the embroidery was generally worked in cross stitch or petit point on hessian, using hard, long staple wool coloured with vegetable dyes. Cream or black silk was also sometimes used to fill in the background or to highlight portions of the work. For work such as this, the design was drawn onto the hessian and then filled in with stitches. Beautiful urns and baskets of flowers resembling Dutch flower paintings were worked in this way, many showing the new varieties of bulbs developed at this time. Classical subjects were also popular, inspired by the new Palladian houses. The agricultural reforms were reflected in charming pastoral needleworks in which well dressed shepherdesses and attentive gentlemen shepherds disport themselves in ordered and idyllic landscapes, generally a large country house can be seen in the background.

As the century progressed, new influences came into play. The displaced rural poor moved into towns where their living conditions were considerably worse than in the country. They provided a ready workforce for the first rumblings of the Industrial Revolution. Merchants and industrialists with growing wealth wanted to climb the social ladder and numerous female academies were opened to teach their daughters the accomplishments necessary for any aspirant to gentility.

High on the list of desirable skills was embroidery, one of the hallmarks of a lady of taste and refinement. First the regulation sampler had to be stitched and then the young pupils could turn their energies to purely decorative needlework. A new type of embroidery, the silk picture, had become fashionable. A picture was drawn with ink on to a piece of silk and the design filled in with various stitches and delicate shading worked with floss silk or crewel wools. Again the subject matter reflected the current concerns and interests of the period.

A major contribution to the attitudes of that time was made by the French philosopher Jean Jacques Rousseau. He felt that a 'love of embroidery was natural to women', and that they were best educated through a study of the natural world. 'Foliage, fruits, flowers and drapery is all they need to know to create their own embroidery pattern, if they can't find one that suits them.' In response to his dictates, many delicate posies of naturalistic flowers, often tied with trailing pale blue ribbons, were worked. Pictures showing ladies in gardens among the flowers were also extremely popular from about 1780.

As health care improved during the second half of the eighteenth century, more children survived their infancy and motherhood assumed a new importance. Mothers were encouraged to show affection for their children and many paintings of the period show happy family groups. Mothers and daughters became favourite subjects for silk pictures; usually depicted holding hands in a rustic setting.

Other pictures illustrated religious and biblical stories, and even the poor became the subjects of embroidery. Their living conditions both in the towns and the country were appalling and ladies were expected to be charitable and spend some of their time doing good works. This poverty stricken section of society was represented as the 'deserving poor' and they were depicted as God fearing, hardworking and clean, living happily in neat cottages apparently content with their humble occupations.

THE EMERGENCE OF BERLIN WOOLWORK

It is often thought that women designed their own needleworks in the eighteenth and early nineteenth centuries. Some did, but many others bought their silk pictures ready drawn out from embroidery shops which also sold the various shades of floss silk and wool. The coloured Berlin woolwork patterns are supposed to have caused the end of personal creativity but, in fact, most women merely exchanged what was one type of needlework kit for another. Berlin woolwork was taken up with alacrity in Britain and America. To work designs in cross stitch with wool was considerably easier than sewing elaborate silk pictures and being a novel concept, it was interesting to try. A mixture of both types of needlework was done until about 1840. Berlin patterns were expensive to start with, but with the advantage of mass production and machine printed periodicals they were soon available to everyone.

The earliest hand coloured patterns for cross stitch appeared in about 1800. In her book *The Art of Needlework*, published in 1840, the Countess of Wilton tells us that in 1804 a print seller called Phillipson published 'a hand painted design on chequered paper for needlework.' He lived in Berlin and it was a Berlin woman, Madame Wittich, who really saw the possibilities of this new type of pattern. She was a gifted needlewoman and with her husband, who was a print maker and bookseller, they produced hundreds of patterns from about 1810. They commissioned artists to copy popular paintings and engravings and the patterns were then printed onto sturdy paper. The various colours of wool to be used in the final piece of needlework were each given a different symbol which was printed onto the chart, just like today's black and white knitting and sampler charts. The scale was generally smaller than modern designs – normally twenty squares to the inch. Each tiny symbol was then painted over by hand with thick watercolour paint, using a small, square-ended brush. The colour made the charts not only much easier to follow but very appealing in their own right and it is rather surprising that relatively few of them have survived to the present day.

Germany during this time was going through a period of peace and prosperity sometimes known as the Biedmeier Period (1815–1848) named after Eichrodt's poems 'Beidmeiers Liedenlust'. The poems extolled the simple pleasures of life and portrayed the average German citizen as a hearty, honest and decent individual – Berlin patterns produced at this time reflect some of the same sentiments. Many of them show romantic Alpine and rural scenes populated by cheerful country people often wearing national costume. Other patterns are rather more in keeping with modern taste showing classical motifs and geometric designs as well as flowers and animals.

Berlin patterns were not available in Britain in any quantity until 1831 when a Mr Wilks opened his embroidery emporium in London's Regent Street. He imported large numbers of quality handpainted patterns from Germany and also Vienna and Paris where they were now being produced. These patterns were expensive with large ones selling for as much forty pounds each, an enormous sum in those days when a kitchen maid earned ten pounds a year. The shop was a great success and by the time Queen Victoria came to the throne in 1837 the craze

(Previous page) This picture shows a sumptuous arrangement of original Victorian pieces of Berlin woolwork. Some are sewn with beads and pearls and others are embellished with chenille and silk. All are from Linda Gumm's antique shop at Camden Passage, London.

for Berlin woolwork was well under way. By 1840, some 1,400 patterns were in regular use, and were coloured by armies of women and girls working mainly for pin money at home. A similar explosion of interest took place in the USA with patterns becoming available six or seven years later than in Britain. Many women's periodicals published Berlin patterns in the same way as special offers are featured today. The patterns were generally poor quality but they helped to popularize the fashion.

The Victorians took themselves seriously, as can be seen by their paintings and the subjects they chose to embroider. Maybe they needed to in order to cope with all the changes that had taken place since the beginning of the century. From being a rural community, Britain had become 'The Workshop of the World' exporting manufactured goods to all corners of the globe. Enormous new wealth had been created and an unprecedented social upheaval was the result. Perhaps in reaction to the elegance and decadence of the late eighteenth century and the Regency period, attitudes became essentially middle class. Hard work, respectability and domesticity were the Victorian ideals though these were heightened somewhat by romanticism and a rather sickly sentimentality. All were exemplified by the model family of the young Queen Victoria apparently living in connubial bliss with her young husband Albert and raising a large clutch of promising children.

The new wealth meant that large numbers of middle class women were now able to employ servants thus acquiring leisure time which had to be filled. Money gave their husbands new status which might be compromised by a working wife. However, the traditional pastimes of the landed gentry were denied to these suburban women as they had no large households to manage or establishments to run. They probably lived in one of the new houses in the red brick terraces that were built all over Britain, staffed by one or two servants at the most.

The variety of the social calendar that makes up the season was beyond them since class barriers were very strong in those days. These women could bear and rear children, submissively cherish their patriarch husbands, visit each other, do some gentle gardening or work for church and charity events. This left quite a lot of free time which could be admirably filled by doing the new Berlin embroidery and other sorts of fancy work. To be able to embroider conferred a certain social standing, it was regarded as a ladylike activity. The results of their labours could be used to embellish their new homes, provide a topic of conversation when visiting, or be sold at charity bazaars to raise money for the 'benighted heathen' and various other good causes.

Berlin woolwork was easy to do and needed very little artistic talent. The colours could be well chosen or impossibly garish but the end result, a piece of needlework, could still be achieved. It was a very soothing and satisfying pastime and the results of their labours are still appreciated today, both for their decorative value and for the fascinating insight they give of life in a different era.

THE NINETEENTH-CENTURY MATERIALS

When the German patterns were first imported, German wool, from the fleeces of Merino sheep which were kept in large flocks in Saxony, was too. It was sometimes called zephyr wool and was a soft, short staple 4-ply wool resembling nylon baby wool in feel and texture. It virtually took over from the long staple, hard worsted-spun wool – crewel wool – which had been used up to that time.

Aniline dyes were developed in the middle of the nineteenth century. Zephyr wool was easy to dye and so bright shades of wool became available for the first time. Brilliant colours such as magenta, emerald green, crimson and yellow were all mixed together to create the strident, detailed compositions so characteristic of Berlin woolwork.

Woolwork pieces showing their original colours are far too garish and bright for most people's taste today. Fortunately, most of them have become dimmed with exposure to sunlight over the years. The different colours have faded at different rates, so that reds and greens have tended to hold their colour, while purples, blues and yellows became very muted. This mixture of soft and brilliant colour is typical of original Berlin woolwork and any attempt to create a modern version must take it into account.

Berlin work was worked on a variety of materials. Earlier pieces tend to be finer and more delicately coloured, and were usually worked on a small meshed silk canvas available in various colours. The background was often left unworked as this type of canvas is reasonably attractive when left bare.

Sometimes the canvas was attached to a piece of flannel and the stitches worked through both layers of fabric. The canvas threads were then pulled out when the design was finished leaving the picture apparently embroidered on the flannel.

Strong brown jute canvas was used for items which needed to withstand everyday use such as chair seats or carpets. Occasionally, perforated paper or painted fine wire mesh were used as base materials for small objects. Later examples of Berlin woolwork are almost universally worked on double or Penelope canvas invented in the 1830s. It was strong and easy to cover and could be used for both gros and petit point; sometimes both were used in the same design. Normally, the background area was filled in with stitches in a plain colour. This was usually black, red or dark blue, although in earlier work, cream, tan, coral or pale blue were more common. It is noticeable that the black wool faded particularly badly, and in many of the backgrounds in which it was used it appears to be olive green. Also, large areas often appear striped or patchy as the different batches of wool used in covering them faded at different rates and to various degrees. To highlight part of the design, raw silk, which is cream in colour, was sometimes used. Small groups of coloured beads could be attached with linen thread to add variety, and sometimes these French beads were used to work the complete pattern. As beads don't fade, the bright colours originally chosen by the nineteenth-century maker can still be seen. In some other pieces, the design was worked with a mixture of gray, white and transparent beads only, a style known as *grisaille*.

Another interesting variation of texture was achieved by the use of plush stitch in which a series of loops of wool were made, each held in place by a cross stitch. The loops were cut after the piece was finished so that the worked area resembled thick velvet or carpet pile. Sometimes the plush work was cut professionally and some magnificently sculptured effects were achieved. Three-dimensional flowers, animals and birds were often created in this way. Sometimes the animals were given glass eyes to make them even more life like.

POPULAR PICTORIAL SUBJECTS

While few patterns are still in existence, a large numbers of Berlin pieces have survived to the present day. As a result, we have some idea which subjects Victorian ladies found most appealing and worked most frequently.

Flowers have always been favourite subjects for embroidery. The bright, fresh colours and endless variety of their shapes and forms lend themselves to replication with the delicate shades and textures of wool and silk. The Victorian patterns of flowers are extremely pretty, especially the early hand-painted designs which show detailed and accurate representations of many different varieties of blooms. They were modelled on paintings and engravings of the time. Roses, with their buds and leaves occur in almost every pattern, sometimes alone, but more often mixed with other flowers. Many of these are hothouse species, newly discovered in plant-hunting expeditions and cultivated in conservatories. They were mixed with the traditional English cottage garden flower varieties such as violets, auriculas, pansies, tulips, poppies and lilies.

Flowers are shown arranged in many different ways (wreaths and posies were popular) and were worked on every sort of object that the ingenious pattern makers could think of to suggest to their customers as possible projects. Sometimes, different flowers were shown entwined into long ropes and garlands and these could be used for pelmets, bell pulls or carpet borders while flowered swags could be made into curtain ties. Large pictures were often made showing very decorative baskets or urns of flowers and these subjects are now especially popular with twentieth-century collectors and decorators. Countless lovely flowered cushions were stitched and can be seen displayed in almost every issue of the decorating magazines over the last few years: a tribute to their timeless charm.

Classical design was used as the inspiration for many embroideries in the early part of the nineteenth century. The Greek key design was popular, as were acanthus leaves, masks, medallions and small repeated abstract motifs. Some of these repeating designs were further elaborated later in the century when large numbers of geometric patterns were produced. I find them fascinating, they are so simple and yet so effective.

Less attractive subjects are the detailed representations of famous paintings. It is sometimes said that before the beginning of the Arts and Crafts movement in the 1880s, the Victorians had no taste of

BANNER SCREEN IN LEVIATHAN

their own but just supported the revival of one historic style after another. Certainly the period from 1830 to 1860 was dominated by an interest in romantic medieval subjects epitomized in print by the novels of Sir Walter Scott. Pictures of his heroes and heroines were often made into Berlin patterns. Rob Roy, the Fair Maid of Perth, and Mary Queen of Scots saying goodbye to Black Douglas were all popular subjects. Painting tended to be on a grandiose scale at that time and needlework versions were often made the same size or larger than the original works. I have seen an example of 'The Death of the Black Prince' which measured over 7× 6ft (2.1×1.8m). It was an awe-inspiring achievement but rather too overwhelming for use in a house today. The work of the popular artist Edwin Landseer, the prints of Baxter or Le Blond and Edward Lear's lithographs were all used to create elaborate patterns. Some were decorative while others were widely regarded as hideous, even in the time when they were worked.

The Victorian Royal family was idolized as a perfect example of domestic felicity and patterns taken from their portraits were popular and have a certain charm. The young Prince Edward makes an appealing subject either alone or with his mother, Queen Victoria. Prince Albert and the young Queen were often worked as a pair of portraits and some enchanting designs show members of the Royal family with their pets. One, showing the child Victoria talking to a parrot, with her terrier at her feet, is very well known. A special range of designs was produced for the American market whose subjects included portraits of George Washington and Abraham Lincoln, and scenes from popular American novels such as *Uncle Tom's Cabin.*

Another widely used source of inspiration for designs are representations of animals and birds. These translated well into Berlin patterns and original worked examples of these subjects are very much collected. Dogs, cats and exotic birds were the most popular subjects but proud stags, lions, tigers and even rabbits and guinea pigs were all used as subjects, and eagles were popular in America.

The observance of religious practice was very strict in Victorian households. Family prayers presided over by the head of the house were a daily ritual. On Sundays, all toys and everyday amusements were put away. One of the few distractions allowed between church services was the sewing of religious scenes in needlework. Thousands of complex and detailed representations of bible stories have survived but as they are of very little interest to collectors they tend to hang about in dusty corners of antique shops. No doubt their time will come. Certainly, canvases printed with versions of Leonardo da Vinci's last supper, not unlike their Victorian predecessors, still sell steadily today.

CREATING A VICTORIAN ATMOSPHERE

Every conceivable type of object was stitched for the Victorian home from the usual cushions, pictures and chair seats to huge carpets that would cover a drawing room floor. These were either made in one piece or from squares of needlework joined together. Further decorative effect could be obtained from woolwork pelmets, bell pulls and curtain ties. Beaded pole screens and banners protected the needlewoman's face from the fire while she worked and she could put her bits and pieces into embroidered pockets hung on the wall. All these items would be massed together in richly papered rooms crowded with ornate furniture and knick knacks. The original unfaded colours must have made the effect quite overwhelming.

Berlin work was also used for making smaller objects which could be given as presents or sold in bazaars. Papa was provided with plaid comforters, smoking caps, waistcoats, cigar cases and very attractive slippers. Friends would be given purses and pin cushions, reticules, tea cosies, spectacle cases and book covers to mention just a few ingenious objects that ladies' magazines suggested to their readers. These items must have been great fun to make and though we might laugh at some of them, Victorian taste really did have a tremendous vitality.

Some of the work is extremely pretty and it is certainly a marvellous source of inspiration. The best of Victorian style is back in vogue, especially in the form of fabrics and wallpaper reproduced from original documents and archives. We no longer have the crowded rooms and overstuffed sofas for which Berlin work was designed but selected pieces can look very well in modern interiors providing a softening and enriching effect.

(Opposite) A collection of original Berlin charts featuring a typical mixture of Victorian designs including religious subjects, flowers and animals.

CHAPTER ONE

VICTORIAN ANIMALS

(Previous page) Victorian
designs do not necessarily
have to go into a Victorian
room scheme. These parrots
– both feathered and stitched
– look well in a modern
conservatory surrounded by
suitably exotic flowers and
fruit.

The fashion for collecting Victorian woolwork animals in the early 1980s led me to produce my needlework kits. I had just sold yet another woolwork spaniel when a collector idly suggested that I start making some kits of these Victorian animals. Her comment made possible an ambition I had been vaguely mulling over for some years. The comment was made in March 1986 and the first kit, needless to say a spaniel, was launched in October of the same year. Since then, I have been able to preserve many patterns and designs which have been becoming increasingly rare and it is now possible for anyone to own a 'Victorian' piece of needlework, even if they do have to make it for themselves.

In 1986, the collectors of needlework animals were very selective. They did not want any old embroidered beast, they were looking for specific types of creatures. The most popular were dogs, especially spaniels sitting on cushions, the bigger and brighter the better. Second came cats, in particular those rather primitive cats made in the first thirty years of the nineteenth century. Many people find them ugly but they project a sort of essence of catness and although simple in design are both visually effective and very decorative.

Lions, tigers and leopards, often worked in long and short stitch rather than cross stitch, had a small fanatical following, mainly among men. Anything really unusual like mice, elephants, rabbits and pigs or extra fluffy sheep was greeted with appreciation, but for no apparent reason other animals were virtually ignored. Deer were dismissed and horses only tolerated; parrots were bought but as a decorative accessory rather than a collectable item, and peacocks were virtually unsaleable as they were reputed to be unlucky.

Some of the rarer pieces of Victorian animal needlework were probably designed by the ladies who made them. Most of them were done at the beginning of the nineteenth century when Berlin patterns were still scarce. Needlewomen had probably seen the new embroidery but had not yet been able to find a pattern they wanted to work. Impatient to begin, they made their own, taking inspiration from the prints and engravings of the time. These early pieces often have a fresh, slightly primitive feel, and were worked in hard, vegetable-dyed wool on coarse but good quality hessian.

The professionally printed and painted patterns of animals were very popular, especially after the zoological gardens in Regents Park was opened in 1828. Brightly coloured tropical birds and all sorts of exotic animals were seen by many people for the first time. Animals such as elephants, lions, tigers and monkeys were represented on patterns, but only a modest number seem to have been worked. It was the colourful parrots, cockatoos, golden pheasants and peacocks that really appealed to the majority of needlewomen. They made perfect subjects for embroidery with their bright, distinctly shaded plummage. Many of the patterns were inspired by Edward Lear's book *Illustrations of the Family Psittercidae or Parrots*, published in 1832, as it was lavishly illustrated with hand coloured lithographs.

The parrot design featured in this chapter was based on a finely worked early Victorian needlework picture. Its inspiration was probably one of the Edward Lear illustrations. The book was also the most likely source of a pair of parrot patterns that were published in the December 1871 and the January 1872 issues of *A Ladies Journal*. A nineteenth-century needlewoman, W. Higgs, combined the two designs into one, showing the birds facing each other. She then worked them as a picture in Madras, East India, in 1891. This picture now hangs in our sitting room over the fireplace still framed in its original maple veneered moulding. The black background has faded to a patchy olive green but it is still a very decorative and attractive piece.

Other books that provided material for the Berlin woolwork designs were John Gould's *Birds of Australia* and his monogram about Toucans. Audubon's *Birds of America* was also a rich source, especially for American patterns. With books of such quality to copy, it is not surprising that the patterns taken from their illustrations are generally superb.

Another source of inspiration was the work of Sir Edwin Landseer (1802–1873). His fine studies of animals brought him to the notice of the Queen and many of his best paintings are still owned by the Royal family. He painted the royal pets, notably Dash, who was a small King Charles Spaniel belonging to the young Queen Victoria. Dash is usually shown sitting in a basket or on an elaborate cushion. The various high quality patterns of him that were produced were used over and over again during the nineteenth century. The charm of the resulting needleworks makes them a favourite 'find' of collectors and decorators. There is a very fine example in the Victoria and Albert Museum, London, and another version is included in this book.

Another frequently seen and attractive Victorian pattern was based on Landseer's painting of a group of Queen Victoria's pets. A red macaw is shown sitting on a perch with two lovebirds while the dogs Islay and Tilco play below. This pattern is usually found worked on fine silk canvas and all the examples I have seen show a very high standard of workmanship. As the pattern is large it would have been expensive and was probably only bought by comparatively well-off and experienced needlewomen.

Further patterns were produced from some of Landseer's other well known paintings. 'Dignity and Impudence' shows a blood hound and a terrier at the entrance to a kennel; 'A distinguished member of the Humane Society' is a portrait of a seated Newfoundland dog called Paul Pry; a much stitched pattern was taken from 'The Monarch of the Glen' which portrays a proud stag in a misty Scottish glen. Most of the needleworks worked from these designs seem to have been large pieces and though impressive do not have the charm of the portraits of Dash.

Foxes appear to have fascinated Victorian needlewomen and a small pattern showing three fox heads was embroidered on all sorts of unlikely items, especially on the front of men's slippers, much to the disapproval of Mrs Merifield who wrote in the *The Journal* in 1851: 'The head of a dog or fox is made to cover the front of a slipper, yet how absurd, not to say startling, is the effect produced by the head of one of these animals protruding from beneath the trousers of a sportsman.' The pattern was probably more often worked by needlewomen living in the suburbs than the wives of fox hunters. Maybe they felt that their husbands could join the hunting set if they had foxes on their slippers. I own a fine example of a woolwork fox clasping a dead duck. This theme, though true to nature is rather unfortunate from a decorating point of view. The fox is worked against a geometric background in three shades of red.

My first designs – a set of twelve – were based on some of the favourite animal subjects that appear in Victorian needleworks. Needless to say they include Dash, seated elegantly in a basket. Other designs in the series feature cats – 'The Contented Cat' and 'The Cream Cat' and two more dogs – 'The Spotted Dog' and 'Toby', a pug. Of this early collection, only

'The Parrot' is featured in this book – the other four animal charts were painted specially for it. The twelve earlier designs and the new ones are all the same size and so could be used together to make an animal carpet, or made up as a set of pictures or cushions.

THE PARROT

Parrots were popular subjects for needlework in the nineteenth century. They were fashionable as pets and their brightly coloured plumage translated well into the brilliant shades of the new Berlin wool.

Queen Victoria's pets were often portrayed in needlework and among them can be seen a magnificent red macaw. Other patterns show cockatoos, love birds and many species of parrots. The birds are shown perched on parrot stands or on the edge of baskets, while others sit on leafy branches or among exotic creepers. The chart makers painted some

The bright colours used in this design provide wide scope for unusual background colours – pale blue or butter yellow look good with the exotic plumage of the bird (the chart is on page 24).

(Overleaf) A sofa piled high with needlework cushions featuring numerous different animal designs ranging from a brightly coloured parrot (see chart on page 24) to a more muted and stylized cat (see chart on page 39).

birds at rest and others with wings outstretched just about to land on a conveniently placed twig.

This parrot is one of the twelve designs that make up my Victorian animals collection. The chart is stylish and I felt the bright colours of the feathers would provide stitchers with a welcome break from sewing large expanses of various shades of brown fur. Most mammals are brown or beige in colour and the red and blue wool makes an attractive change.

It took some time to find a suitable authentic nineteenth-century parrot to adapt. Most Victorian pieces featuring these birds are particularly large and ornate and I was looking for a much more compact and modest bird. I think that a certain amount of artistic license was taken with the plumage of the original example that I eventually found. My daughter Anna who is a parrot enthusiast has not been able to track down the exact species in any of her parrot books – she says it is a macaw with its tail chopped off and funny coloured feathers.

This attractive, though unidentified, bird is very popular. He seems to appeal especially strongly to men who, when asked at shows which design they like best, usually choose him immediately. I know he is fun to work and although the pattern looks complicated, it in fact progresses quite easily.

The parrot is a highly decorative design and looks well against many background colours. The original was set against a cream background but black, pale blue or butter yellow also look good. He will enhance all sorts of rooms but settles especially happily as a cushion in a study or library armchair. Framed in maple, he also makes a splendid picture such as that which is seen on page 19 and he is part of a carpet on pages 131 and 161. The photograph shows him in a conservatory surrounded by all sorts of suitably spiky tropical plants, altogether a very adaptable bird.

THE PARROT
YARN COLOURS AND QUANTITIES

The quantities are the number of yards of Elizabeth Bradley wool needed for each square of 160×160 stitches worked on 10 mesh canvas in cross stitch. (See page 164 for skein lengths of different brands.)

Key

1	E10	25
2	A6	23
3	A5	23
4	E3	18
5	C6	18
6	C3	6
7	H5	12
8	G3	17
9	H1	12
10	C1	7
11	I10	21
12	I7	35
13	D10	28
14	I3	26
15	H10	6
16	H8	6
17	B6	3
18	L3	4
19	L5	18
20	L7	11

Background: 8 hanks

RABBITS

This is my third attempt at painting a rabbit pattern: I persevered as I particularly wanted to design one – rabbits are such very appealing animals. Pieces of Victorian woolwork depicting them are rare, and I was not lucky enough to find a suitably attractive example to act as inspiration. My first two efforts finished up looking like a cross between fluffy toys and Bugs Bunny and I must admit that I am rather pleased to have at last produced reasonably convincing animals.

The aim of the photography in this book was to show needlework in many different settings, thus providing ideas for its use. The early Victorians were fond of building all sorts of exotic summer houses, grottos and Gothic cottages, even Chinese pavilions or romantic ruins were constructed, and all added interest to nineteenth-century gardens. Rustic log cabins were one of the most popular types and were often furnished with benches, tables and chairs all made from logs to match the walls. Inventive potters made huge tree trunk plant pots out of stoneware with all sorts of holes from which ferns and creepers could sprout. Tobacco jars, biscuit barrels and umbrella stands were made to match.

Twigginess in general was fashionable and even pictures and mirrors were surrounded by mock twig frames. Here a rustic frame for the rabbit picture has been made and hung on a log cabin wall with a birch

(Opposite) These rabbits nestling in a leafy woodland hollow seem to need a special frame. This one has been made from twigs and moss with oak leaves, acorns and old man's beard. A log cabin background completes the picture.

trunk shelf below.

Remnants of the twig and log craze are still with us today and rustic summer houses, garden seats, and pots can still be brought at garden centres. The rabbit design made into a cushion or picture would sit happily on such furniture or in any country cottage setting. It could be framed conventionally in a maple frame or with a moulding painted to look like wood with one of the faux wood finishes. Alternatively you could have a rabbit picture framed with nuts, oak leaves and moss, just like this one.

RABBITS
YARN COLOURS AND QUANTITIES

The quantities are the number of yards of Elizabeth Bradley wool needed for each square of 160×160 stitches worked on 10 mesh canvas in cross stitch. (See page 164 for skein lengths of different brands.)

Key		
1	N1	3
2	N3	4
3	N4	4

4	K3	10
5	K5	28
6	K6	48
7	J8	54
8	I9	30
9	J6	25
10	I4	54
11	J4	20
12	C11	24
13	A9	6
14	G9	10
15	G8	17
16	G6	17
17	F8	24
18	G4	18
19	E4	18
20	F6	11
21	F5	11
22	D11	8
23	F11	25
24	F10	50
25	I3	8
26	I2	20
27	C2	8
28	D2	7
29	C1	8
30	H4	31
31	H2	20
32	H1	18
33	F3	12

DASH THE SPANIEL

I feel that this book would not have been complete without Queen Victoria's famous pet spaniel Dash, unusually he is shown standing rather than sitting on his cushion. Most of the Victorian patterns of Dash were based on a painting by Landseer, but mine is adapted from a rather moth-eaten nineteenth-century Berlin woolwork picture. The spaniel it showed was a lighter dog than is usual and probably came from different source material.

I decided to paint him against a darkly striped background as an experiment. To a certain extent, I find that the range of colours I use depends on the time of year, and as I painted this chart in February when it was cold and dark, my preference was for rich, warm and mellow colours. The piece was then made up to fit a Victorian mahogony firescreen,

taking over two months to complete, by which time it was spring. By then, my range of colours had moved on to a lighter and clearer palette so, to my mind, the spaniel now looked rather dark. As a result, I had another version made, but this time against a rich green background which makes a good alternative. I also combined Dash the Spaniel with the Tassel Border (see page 121) and covered a square box stool with the completed piece. Both needleworks have been placed in an untidy man's study for the photograph on page 31: this room looks very comfortable to me; as I like a lot of clutter around me when I am working.

Original examples of these little woolwork spaniels are extremely collectable, fetching good prices

Spaniel woolworks were often used to cover stools and firescreens (see overleaf). To me, the rich colours of this little dog suggested a comfortable and cluttered library setting.

(Overleaf) Many little girls are horse enthusiasts and this Victorian child's bedroom is enriched by two Palamino pony woolworks. One has been worked on a black background and made into a cushion and the other has been set against pale blue stripes and makes a delightful picture (the striped background is one of a selection of background charts on page 79).

in salerooms if they are large in size and of good quality workmanship. They are very popular with antique dealers and interior decorators, adding a touch of charm to practically any room scheme.

Although the actual spaniels themselves are invariably worked in shades of grays or browns, the appearance of the finished pieces can be varied by changing the colour of the background area. A spaniel with a peach or pale blue background would look pretty in a bedroom; if set against a black or dark green background he would suit a library.

DASH THE SPANIEL
YARN COLOURS AND QUANTITIES

The quantities are the number of yards of Elizabeth Bradley wool needed for each square of 160×160 stitches worked on 10 mesh canvas in cross stitch. (See page 164 for skein lengths of different brands.) Quantities have not been provided for the striped background (key colours 1, 15 and 16), however, as you may wish to plan you own.

Key		
1	G7	1
2	E12	41
3	E9	19
4	E8	26
5	F9	32
6	E5	3
7	F6	8
8	E2	1
9	E1	23
10	C1	23
11	F3	36
12	N11	8
13	N8	49
14	N7	13
15	I9	
16	D11	7

Background: 9 hanks

THE PALAMINO HORSE

Considering the importance of the horse in the western world before the invention of the internal combustion engine, and the numbers of superb paintings of horses produced over the last three hundred years, it is surprising how few horse patterns were produced for Berlin woolwork. Perhaps horses

were not romantic enough subjects.

Of those which were charted, a number were set in desert landscapes, with often a dashing, Sheik-like figure in flowing robes shown astride the rearing or cavorting steed. Others show the Royal Children riding their ponies.

I have seen and owned a number of pieces of woolwork featuring a small, neat, Palamino pony. He is usually worked against a duck-egg blue background and is always stitched in shades of creamy, beige wool. Recently, a kind customer from Norfolk sent me photographs of an original woolwork of this horse in her possession. It shows some interesting variations. For instance, the pony is worked in plush stitch instead of the more usual cross stitch. This stitch achieves the effect of a thick pile carpet, and the ends of wool have been cut to echo the contours of the horse so that he stands out realistically from his background. He has been placed in a circus ring instead of the usual desert or parkland scene and a red and yellow harness has been added to complete the picture. He has been worked against a rich red background rather than the more usual pale blue. This is a delightful piece of needlework, very rich in colour and extremely decorative. It is also interesting in that it gives some idea as to how changes can be made to a basic pattern to make it more individual.

For instance, the colour of the horse could be changed from a palamino, into, say, a chestnut, by using shades of rusty brown wool instead of creams and beiges. Alternatively, the mane and tail could be sewn in brown and black wool and the body in tan to suggest a bay.

Your own version of the pony can be set against a whole variety of coloured backgrounds which could be either plain or patterned. I think that the pale blue striped background shown in the photograph is very effective.

THE PALAMINO HORSE
YARN COLOURS AND QUANTITIES

The quantities are the number of yards of Elizabeth Bradley wool needed for each square of 161×161 stitches worked on 10 mesh canvas in cross stitch. (See page 164 for skein lengths of different brands.)

Key		
1	I8	34
2	I4	28

1 2 3 4 5 6 7 8 9 10 11 12 13

3	J8	10
4	J5	11
5	J3	8
6	G7	3
7	E11	3
8	E8	3
9	G4	8
10	E4	28
11	E3	21
12	E1	32
13	F5	24

Background: 8 hanks

THE TABBY CAT

This tabby cat design is very characteristic of a
whole group of interesting early nineteenth-century
feline needleworks in which the embroidered cats
are invariably shown sitting on tasselled cushions or
simple footstools. The finished pieces are usually
quite small in size and are normally either framed as
pictures or mounted on little nineteenth-century
stools. All these woolworks have a primitive and
rather stylized air and fit well into kitchens and
country rooms, the austere lines of American and
British county furniture complementing the simple

outline and basic shading of the cats.

As a category of needleworks, they are well loved
by decorators and the antique trade and because
of their charm they often command a high price.
Several antique dealers that I know have their own
small collections. The original piece from which
The Tabby Cat is derived was worked in fine wool.
It was the first antique needlework piece that I kept
for myself, and it is still one of my favourites.

The original piece is quite small and to make it
bigger without losing the essential simplicity, I
changed each stitch into a group of four and if the
design is worked on 10 mesh canvas in cross stitch,
a tabby cat like those shown in the country kitchen
opposite can be made. If, however, you would like
a smaller and daintier tabby cat, just reduce each
group of four stitches back to one. The finished
piece will then measure 80 stitches by 80 stitches,
rather than 160 by 160. Cats like these were sometimes worked on samplers of the 1830s and 1840s.
Stitched in fine wool or silk onto linen they look
very charming.

If you prefer, a ginger cat can easily be made instead of a tabby by using three shades of rusty orange
wool instead of the grays and blacks. The nose, eyes
and whiskers would, of course, remain the same,

though. This is a good design for a beginner to work, as the chart is easy to follow and the resulting cat is showy and distinctive. I feel he is a little too primitive in type to be included with the other animals in a carpet, but he makes very decorative cushions and pictures.

THE TABBY CAT
YARN COLOURS AND QUANTITIES

The quantities are the number of yards of Elizabeth Bradley wool needed for each square of 160×160 stitches worked on 10 mesh canvas in cross stitch.

(See page 164 for skein lengths of different brands.)

Key

1	G11	24
2	H4	23
3	H2	32
4	F4	25
5	C6	7
6	C2	24
7	E3	28
8	B6	21
9	B2	10
10	I9	2

Background: 9 hanks

Background colours can be chosen not only to complement the design itself, but also to enhance the room in which the finished piece will be set. This cat has been worked against dark blue.

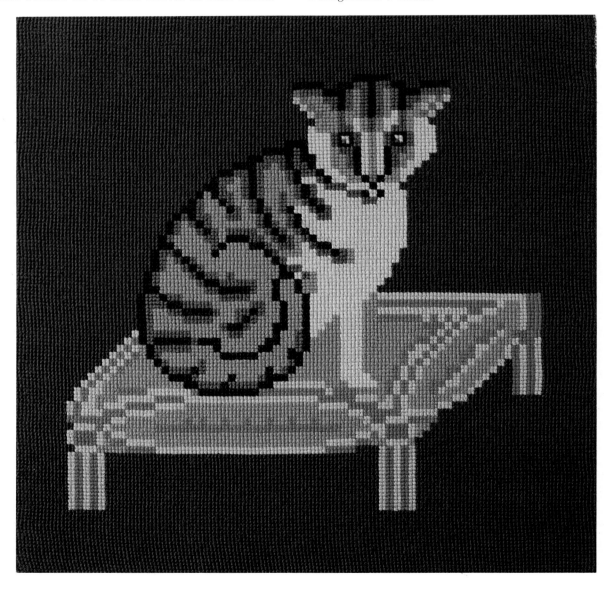

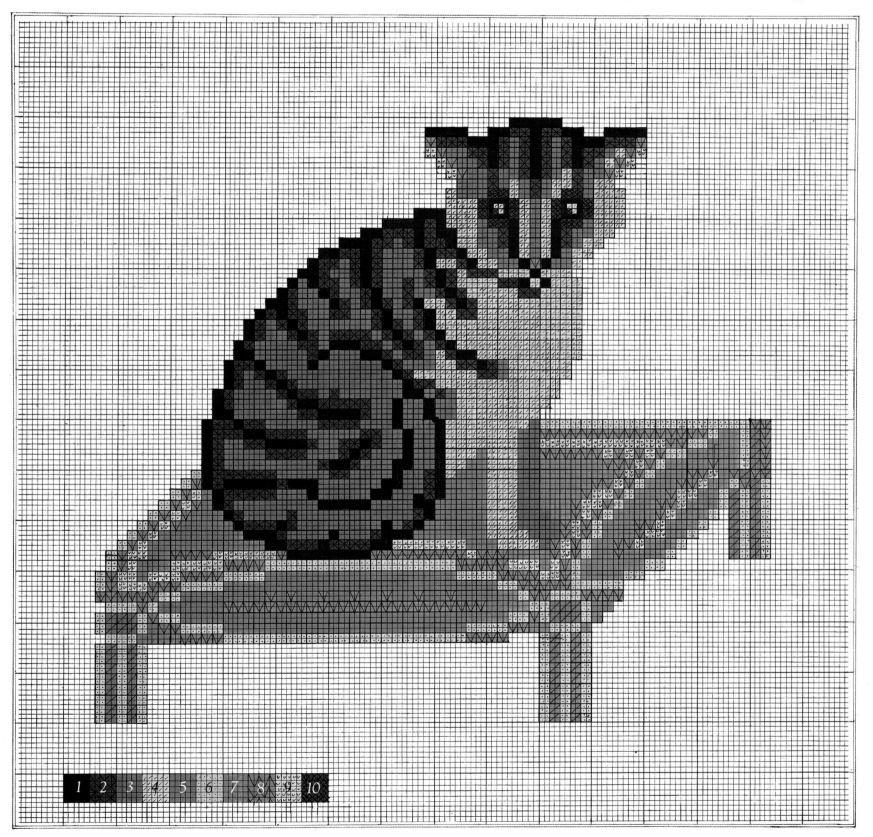

CHAPTER TWO

DESIGNS WITH FLOWERS

(Previous page) Roses are almost the hallmark of Victorian needlework and I felt that this book would not have been complete without a selection of rose designs. This Wreath of Roses (see chart on page 48) holds many of my favourite varieties and looks fresh and pretty worked on a cream background as shown here.

Victorian ladies loved to embroider flowers and many of the pieces of Berlin woolwork that have survived show brightly coloured posies, wreaths and garlands of flowers. This nineteenth-century enthusiasm for flowering plants was caused by a combination of the natural human love of growing things and a mixture of social and historic events. The Industrial Revolution and the growth of the middle classes led to a building boom and every Englishman wanted his own 'castle' with its matching garden, however small.

Britain is a land of gardens. For hundreds of years plants have been cultivated for their beauty and their scent or as a source of food and medicines. Garden styles have changed over the years and tend to alternate between an ideal of symmetrical formality and organized naturalness. Medieval herb enclosures and Tudor knot gardens developed into the elaborate parterres of the Renaissance and Restoration period, while eighteenth-century gardens favoured a studied wildness. Trees and shrubs were planted so that the garden looked as much like a natural landscape as possible. Flowers, when cultivated at all, were scattered among the trees or grown in informal borders. As the century progressed an increasing number of specimen plants were brought into the country from abroad. Botanic gardens and nurseries were started and many new plants became available every year.

This proliferation of choice escalated towards the end of the century and continued in the first half of the nineteenth century. There was what amounted to a virtual explosion of the numbers of species, hybrids and varieties of flowering plants that could be obtained. Flowers were suddenly in demand and gardening was the fashion. Nurserymen eager for new species to offer their customers sent plant collectors out to as many corners of the globe as they could possibly reach.

Many of the plants grown in British gardens today are the result of these expeditions. Ribes, lupins, salvias, fuchsias and clarkias came from North America, and petunias and verbena from the Argentine. India produced *Clematis montana*, *Tulipa stellata* and *Primula denticulata* among many others. China was a rich source of specimens, too, many of them collected by missionaries. Several captains of the East India Company acquired plants when buying silks and teas and many beautiful roses, the wisteria,

camellias and magnolias were brought to Britain by this route. The nineteenth century was also the age of hybridization. There was great interest in producing bigger and better examples of existing flowers, florist flowers as they are sometimes called.

Popular subjects for the art of hybridization were auriculas, carnations, tulips and pansies. Precise codes of properties were demanded for each flower, detailing the size, form and colour. Ideally, the shape of the bloom should be regular with a circular form and the size as large as possible. The minimum size of a carnation, for instance, had to be 2½ inches (6.25cm) in diameter and some were as large as 4 inches (10cm) across.

Before the nineteenth century, flowers played a minor part in garden design but as the century progressed the garden became a showplace to display all the wide variety of flowering plants available. John Loudon, the author of *The Gardener's Magazine*, advocated that the garden be divided into different sections, each suited to the type of plant to be grown in it. Shrubs and small trees should be confined to a shrubbery or wilderness; damp loving plants to a bog garden, and alpines could be cultivated in crevices between artistically arranged heaps of boulders, or rockeries as they came to be called.

Many of the newly discovered species were not fully hardy in Britain, and so they needed to be raised under glass before being planted out to flower all summer long. Examples such as zinnias, marigolds and lobellia were put out each spring into geometric beds set in either grass or gravel. Roses were popular, especially the new semiperpetual bourbon roses, so often stitched into Victorian woolworks. They were grown in elaborate rose gardens where they could be planted in ordered ranks, trained into standard forms, or encouraged to tumble from rustic trellises.

This surprisingly modern approach to garden planting was only supported to a limited extent. Shrubberies and rock gardens were certainly constructed, but far the most popular style of Victorian garden featured an elaborate system of shaped beds reminiscent of a Tudor knot garden. These beds would be edged with neat box hedges or special edging tiles and filled with a succession of regimented and brightly coloured flowers throughout the year.

Further elaboration was provided by the addition of sun dials and artistically positioned statues and fountains. Romantic ivy-covered grottos and arbours could fill a dull corner. The *Floricultural Magazine* in 1841 tells us that:

'Hermitages and caves are also interesting when proper situations are chosen: in these could be kept a small collection of books calculated for private study and the furniture of this sequestered retreat should be exactly of that simple and useful nature as would be suitable to a recluse.'

Further indications of the Victorian attention to detail are given in the same article:

'Neat resting places should be placed in different parts, choosing the situation of some in shaded groves, others upon elevated spots .... Much taste may be displayed in the formation of such seats, from the polished temple of Flora, Venus etc to the rude roots of trees and misshapen fragments of rocks or rude stone .... Moss houses of various construction, root houses, Russian, Swedish, Lapland, Scotch and Swiss cottages should be disposed of in situations peculiarly adapted for them.'

Reaction was bound to set in. Although the ostentatious and elaborate gardens must have been enormous fun to plan and lay out, some late nineteenth-century garden writers regarded them with a certain amount of derision. Gertrude Jekyll and William Robinson, among others, felt that plants should once more be grown in a more natural way and the charming informality of cottage gardens was extolled. It was felt that the various species should be arranged to give a harmonious mixture of shape and colour and today we follow similar guidelines but with the addition of some of the more charming features from previous centuries. Topiary and knot gardens are popular once more and Victorian details such as edging tiles, rose arches and statues all have their place again. Like old varieties of flowers, they are too pretty to be ignored.

The majority of nineteenth-century gardeners and plant collectors were male but Victorian ladies were encouraged to take an interest in gardening. In fact, Victorian gardens with their neat beds and gravel paths were particularly suitable for ladies hampered by the long skirts, crinolines and bustles of the period. The pastime was thought to be not only unexceptional and healthy, but beneficial to mental and spiritual welfare. Lessons were drawn from a study of plants and horticulture. The humbleness of the violet, the fading of a beautiful rose, or the business of a bee could all provide useful illustrations of popular Victorian sentiments.

Many gardening magazines and manuals were produced in the nineteenth century, several specifically for ladies. Jane Loudon, the wife of John, wrote *Practical Instructions for Gardening for Ladies* in 1841 in which she gives detailed and practical advice on all aspects of both flower and vegetable gardening. She discusses the number of pot plants to display on a windowsill, the making of a hot bed for melons, and the twelve different varieties of broccoli among many other topics. Another writer, Lydia Johnson went on to express the Victorian view of lady gardeners perfectly in her *Every Lady her own Flower Garden* in 1845:

' ... flower gardening has progressed rapidly, and the amusement of floriculture has become the dominant passion of the ladies of Great Britain. It is a passion most blessed in its effects, considered as an amusement or a benefit. Nothing humanises and adorns the female mind more surely than a taste for ornamental gardening. It compels the reason to act, and the judgement to observe; it is favourable to meditation of the most serious kind; at it exercises the fancy in harmless and elegant occupation, and braces the system by its healthful tendency.'

By the time Queen Victoria ascended the throne, gardening had become highly fashionable, flowers were news and the Victorians with characteristic enthusiasm wanted flowers on everything. Luckily, by the mid years of the nineteenth century there were plenty of entrepreneurs to make sure they got them. Wallpaper, fabrics, carpets and hats all sprouted flowers and foliage to match the elaborate flower filled gardens.

In 1841, Mr Wilks opened his emporium in Regent Street and filled it with German patterns and wool. Berlin woolwork had started its long period of popularity and ladies all over the country settled

*(Previous page) Black
makes a rich and dramatic
background colour for any
needlework design and these
three rings of roses are no
exception. The Wreath of
Roses (see chart on page 48)
and the little moss Rosebud
Wreath (see chart on
page 53) have been made
into pictures. The tiny Rose
Wreath (see chart on page
133) just fitted into the front
of an old black marble clock.*

down to cover their houses with canvas work. In the early years of the craze flower designs were the ones most often embroidered.

Many of the patterns were magnificent, like brightly coloured mosaics, and are highly decorative in their own right. They show different flowers mixed together in bunches, wreaths and garlands regardless of the season. The new varieties and cultivars were popular, lilies, gloxinias, camellias, morning glory and oriental poppies all bloom together in rich and exotic arrangements.

The mixture of flowers was sometimes purely incidental but often each flower was carefully chosen to give meaning to the posy – the language of flowers was a popular concept in Victorian Britain. Each flower was endowed with its own special quality or emotion, the meanings were widely known and complex messages could be sent. Wreaths or bunches of blooms could be painted onto cards or stitched into needlework gifts such as purses or slippers. Tiny flower needleworks were sometimes stuck into scrapbooks or onto frilly beribboned valentines.

Many books and articles were written on the subject. A list from the ladies' magazine *Penelope* in 1826 tells us that:

> 'the rose represents beauty, a rosebud means youth, oakleaves show patriotism, laurel is bravery, violets signify humbleness, pansies friendship. A lily shows innocence and snowdrops happy expectations. Tulips mean pride, daffodils vanity and forget me nots lasting memories.'

Other meanings seem rather more unlikely, a turnip apparently symbolizes charity. According to Marcus Ward's *The Language and Poetry of Flowers*, a marigold worn on the head shows indifference and displayed on the bosom indicates mental anguish. Obviously care had to be taken when deciding which flowers should be worn on a hat. Berlin pictures often show suitable mixtures of flowers like roses, violets, lilies and pansies, meaning beauty, humility, innocence and friendship. I have never yet seen one featuring a turnip.

As many of the artists who designed Berlin patterns worked from popular paintings and engravings, the quality of the pattern depended to a certain extent on the quality of the original work of art. Designers of flower patterns had superb material to

work from in the nineteenth century. The new varieties of flowers were well illustrated in periodicals and books of engravings and their bright colours made them particularly attractive to designers who suddenly had a wide spectrum of new aniline dyed wools at their disposal.

The best known of all flower painters must surely be Joseph Redouté. Born in Luxembourg in 1759 he studied at Kew in his youth and while in England learnt the art of stipple engraving. Back in France he became drawing master to Marie Antoinette and visited her during her captivity in the Temple. It was Josephine de Beauharnais, the wife of Napoleon, who was to be Redouté's greatest and most generous patron and for her he illustrated *Le Jardin de Malmaison*. The roses of Malmaison were painted for the magnificent book *Les Roses* published after her death in 1817.

With such material to work from it is not surprising that many of the Berlin patterns showing roses are so superb. The flowers are shown in every state and shade from plump buds to full-blown magnificence with bourbon roses as the favourites. These fat, round, cabbage roses were the result of a chance cross between a damask and a china rose, in the French island of Reunion. They were semi-perpetual in their flowering habit and the Victorians loved them calling the many varieties that they developed by the most romantic names – Reine de Violettes, Boule de neige and Souvenir de St Anne's are just a few.

Berlin woolwork featuring flowers in general and roses in particular was used to cover every type of Victorian furniture. The brightly coloured bouquets trailing all over balloon backed armchairs, dining chairs and stools must have been quite dazzling in their new and unfaded colours. The effect was sometimes further enriched by the addition of flower strewn needlework carpets, pelmets, pole screens, curtain ties and cushions. Finely worked pictures in gilt frames could be hung on the walls and servants summoned by pulling long, flowered, bell pulls. Certain churchmen, however, finally drew the line. Roses on church kneelers and vestments was going too far and the church architect, Augustus Pugin, insisted that the patterns used in churches should be suitably ecclesiastical.

Roses and other flowers seem to be as popular now as they were in the nineteenth century. Once again there is great enthusiasm for gardening and many beautiful and historic gardens are open to the public. Old fashioned garden styles have been revived and antique varieties of plants rebred and rediscovered. Again this interest is reflected in the home, especially on wallpapers and furnishing fabrics. Many nineteenth-century documents have been reproduced and some of the best Victorian examples of these items are once more available. Not surprisingly, flowered needlework to match is also back in vogue.

Patterns and kits for flower wreaths and posies have always been available but over the years the flower forms in them have tended to become somewhat simplified. The more robust and detailed Victorian flower designs did not always suit earlier twentieth-century decorative styles. More modern needlework designers often turned their attention to fresh ways of representing flowers and many of the results are very attractive. However, there is now a great interest in classic and unsimplified period flower designs that are in keeping with the antique furnishings of many British and American houses. The flower charts in this chapter have been designed with this end in view and are intended to be decorative, useful and enjoyable to work.

A WREATH OF ROSES

'What is more tranquil than a musk rose blowing
In a green island, far from all men's knowing'
Keats

Roses are my favourite flower and I find them hard to resist in any form. Modern varieties bloom for most of the year with gay abandon while older species of roses give their all in one great burst of colour and scent. Victorians loved them and in the language of flowers they symbolized beauty.

Some of the best of the Victorian Berlin charts feature roses. They were inspired by paintings and engravings of the day and are so pretty in their own right that I have them framed as pictures on the wall at home. A book about decorative Victorian needlework would not be complete without a rose pattern and this wreath has been compiled from a number of sources. I used the best of my Victorian charts, several excellent books on roses and my own observations of the flowers growing.

I have tried to capture some of the charm of a few of my favourite varieties. The clear pink and white

stripes of Varigata de Bologna; the simplicity of the Dog rose and its brighter cousin Amy Robsart; the sweet rounded shape of La Reine Victoria, and the soft wine red Cardinal Richlieu are all there. With them is a pink tinged, fully mature flower of Madame Pierre Oger and a luscious, pale peach, half-opened bud of Great Maiden's Blush just about to burst open into full bloom. This wreath of roses would look well worked against many background colours. Perhaps a plain black or cream would be most traditional although a pale blue or creamy yellow would also be pretty. The finished pieces could be made into excellent chair and stool covers as well as the usual pictures and cushions. As the square measures 160 by 160 stitches this piece can be joined with the other floral charts in this book of similar dimensions to make a very pretty needlework carpet.

A WREATH OF ROSES
YARN COLOURS AND QUANTITIES

The quantities are the number of yards of Elizabeth Bradley wool needed for each square of 160×160 stitches worked on 10 mesh canvas in cross stitch. (See page 164 for skein lengths of different brands.)

Key

1	I3	9
2	I4	10
3	J6	19
4	J5	24
5	K5	12
6	K6	9
7	K4	11
8	I7	18
9	I2	15
10	I8	18
11	I10	9
12	C2	6
13	C3	8
14	A3	19
15	A2	18
16	F5	23
17	F6	10
18	E1	10
19	B2	38
20	B3	28
21	B4	13
22	B5	14
23	B6	10

24	A4	32
25	A5	23
26	A6	16
27	A7	10
28	N8	8

Background: 6 hanks

ROSEBUD WREATH

The chart on page 53 shows a wreath of fat, yellow moss rosebuds. In his book *Old Garden Roses* (1936), Edward A Bunyard quotes an excerpt from an old Calvados legend about the birth of the moss rose:

'One day the Angel, who each day brings the dew on her wings, feeling weary asked the Rose for shelter for the night. On awakening she asked how this hospitality might be repaid. The Rose answered "Make me even more beautiful." "What grace," said the Angel, "can I give to thee most beautiful of all flowers?" Meditating on this request, she cast her eyes down to the mossy bed

Here the Wreath of Roses has been stitched with a black background creating a richer effect.

(Previous page) Sometimes, special small cushions are made to carry the rings up the aisle at a wedding. This small pillow, embroidered with a wreath of yellow moss rosebuds, would be delightful for such a purpose.

from which the Rose sprang, and gathering some, placed it on the young buds. Thus was born the Moss Rose.'

The actual origins of this rose are unknown but wherever it came from it was certainly a great favourite in the nineteenth century. It appears on Valentine cards, china, painted trays, fabric and of course, on needlework pieces.

This little wreath can be used alone or with one of the borders shown on the chart to make a big pin cushion or small pillow. Sometimes, wedding rings are carried up the aisle on a small ornate cushion, and the photograph here shows a cushion made for such a purpose. Further embellishments can be added to the design by the use of a patterned background. Narrow stripes would be smart and spots look extremely pretty. They also make the background area more fun to work.

If you do decide to make a pin cushion or small cusion from this design, then work the sides as well as the centre square part of the design. The corners can then be sewn together with small stitches and a square of silk or velvet can be sewn on to the bottom of the box shape to form a base. Traditionally, sawdust or bran was used to fill pin cushions but normal toy stuffing does just as well and it is not as heavy.

The rosebuds on the chart and in the photograph on the previous page are yellow, but they can be sewn in pink wool instead and deep red, peach or white also look pretty. Just work each bud in three shades of the colour that you choose. 'White' buds need white, cream and either a pale gray or a very pale pink as the third colour. The background can be worked in a wide variety of plain colours. Cream and black are shown in this book, but pale blue, peach or bright pink would be pretty. If spots or stripes are wanted they can either be worked in one of the rosebud colours or a contrasting shade. Lilac spots look pretty with pink rosebuds and dark blue spots are chic with red ones.

Small woolwork items make very acceptable presents. As already suggested, this chart could be used to make pin cushions or small pillows for gifts. I like a really big pin cushion myself as I constantly lose things. But if you would prefer a smaller version, just work the design in crewel wool on a smaller mesh canvas than the 10 mesh shown here. By using the borders, a variety of small items could be made.

Belts, braces, camera straps or book marks all make useful gifts.

Samplers are becoming an increasingly popular wedding or christening present. Worked in perle cotton or pure silk on to a natural linen scrim, this design would make a very attractive small sampler. Initials or a heart could be put in the centre of the wreath or a message added below. 'Bless the babe' or 'Welcome little stranger' were often used to convey good wishes in the nineteenth century.

ROSEBUD WREATH
YARN COLOURS AND QUANTITIES

The quantities are the number of yards of Elizabeth Bradley wool needed for each central square of 78× 78 stitches worked on 10 mesh canvas in cross stitch. (See page 164 for skein lengths of different brands.)

CHARTED COLOURWAY (YELLOW)

Key		
1	J8	7
2	K5	9
3	K4	7
4	J6	7
5	J5	9
6	I5	8
7	I2	18
8	C3	11
9	D4	7
10	C2	6

ALTERNATIVE COLOURWAY (PINK)

Key		
1	J8	7
2	K5	9
3	K4	7
4	J6	7
5	J5	9
6	I5	8
7	I2	18
8	B3	11
9	B2	7
10	B1	6
11 (spots)	N1	14

Background: 2 hanks

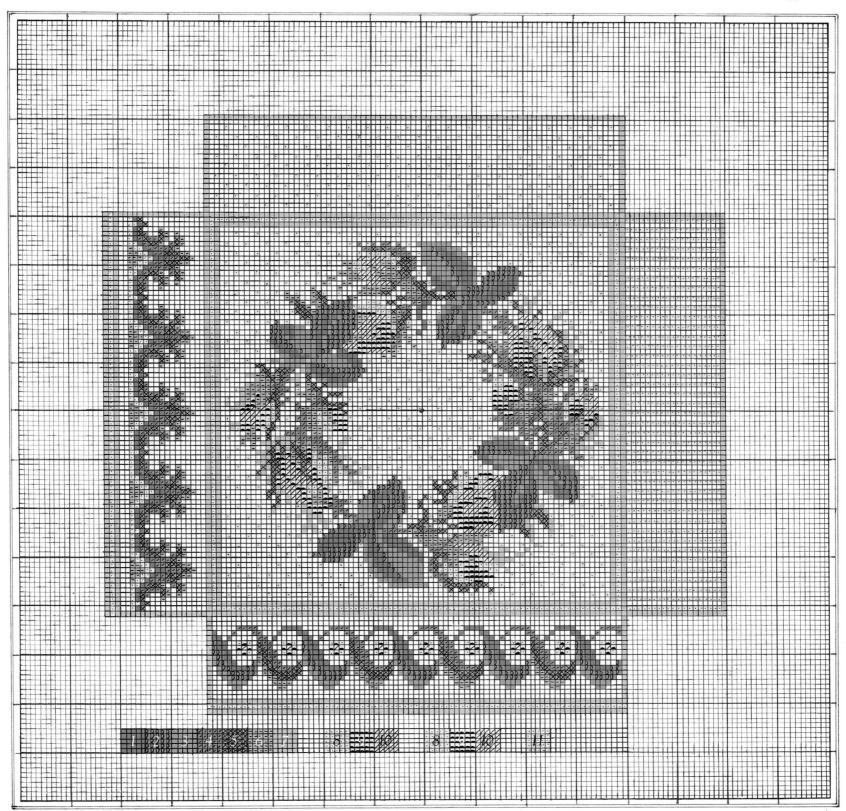

The Rosebud Wreath design can be used without the borders to create a small and charming picture.

BORDER 1 (BOTTOM)

(The quantities are sufficient for all four sides if worked on 10 mesh yarn.)

Key

1	J8	14
2	K5	12
3	K4	7
4	J6	7
5	J5	7
6	I5	6
7	I2	11
8	3	20
9	D4	8
10	C2	2

Background: 2 hanks

BORDER 2 (LEFT SIDE)

(The quantities are sufficient for all four sides if worked on 10 mesh yarn.)

Key

1	J8	11
4	J6	14

5	J5	11
6	I5	18
7	I2	11
8	C3	22

Background: 2 hanks

A ROSE SWAG

What could be prettier in a light sunny drawing room or bedroom than a pelmet and matching curtain ties sewn with roses? The design here shows a semi-circular swag of buds, leaves and flowers which can be adapted for both purposes. The garland is best worked against an area of plain background the shape of which can be varied according to the dimensions of the window or the thickness of the curtains for which the tie-backs are intended.

Woolwork pelmets and curtain ties were particu-larly popular in the nineteenth century. Tie-backs are usually shaped like a sickle moon with blunt ends instead of pointed ones and their length depends on the thickness of the curtain. A heavy velvet, inter-lined curtain needs a longer tie-back than a delicate muslin or silk drape. The tie must not be too tight or the curtain will not hang properly.

To use this rose swag design for a curtain tie it is necessary to extend the background at each end un-til the finished piece is the right length and depth. The shape of the extensions should be rather like a pair of jug handles added to each side of the basic semi-circle and a basic outline is supplied with the chart. The best way to stitch tie-backs is to mark the shape of the tie-back on the canvas before start-ing to sew. Be generous with your margins, in case adjustments need to be made later.

If necessary, the finished pieces of woolwork can

The Rose Swag design is very versatile, it can be easily adapted to create a curtain tie-back or pelmet.

24	A4	32
25	A5	23
26	A6	16
27	A7	10
28	N8	8

Background: 6 hanks

ROSEBUD WREATH

The chart on page 53 shows a wreath of fat, yellow moss rosebuds. In his book *Old Garden Roses* (1936),

Edward A Bunyard quotes an excerpt from an old Calvados legend about the birth of the moss rose:

'One day the Angel, who each day brings the dew on her wings, feeling weary asked the Rose for shelter for the night. On awakening she asked how this hospitality might be repaid. The Rose answered "Make me even more beautiful." "What grace," said the Angel, "can I give to thee most beautiful of all flowers?" Meditating on this request, she cast her eyes down to the mossy bed

Here the Wreath of Roses has been stitched with a black background creating a richer effect.

be stiffened with buckram, and the whole lined with silk or lining fabric. A length of thin cord or piping could be attached around the edge of the tie-back if extra embellishment is needed. Finishing is best done by hand rather than with a sewing machine. Finally, a brass ring should be sewn at each end of the tie-back. They can be looped over hooks suitably positioned on the window frame, to keep the open curtains in place.

Very decorative pelmets, like the one shown in the photograph on page 58, can be made by working one long length of canvas or by joining rose swags together to form a long strip of scalloped woolwork (see page 153 for how to join canvas). Measure the top of your window and then work out on paper how the proposed pelmet will look. Different arrangements of the basic semi-circle are possible but a certain amount of adjustment and experiment may be necessary for the 16-inch swags to fit your window perfectly. Again, the finished piece should be stiffened, lined and then edged with cord or piping if required.

Although such woolwork items would take a considerable time to make they would last many years and could enhance a whole series of pairs of curtains – Victorian pelmets and curtainties are still used today, well over 100 years after they were made.

A ROSE SWAG
YARN COLOURS AND QUANTITIES

The quantities are the number of yards of Elizabeth Bradley wool needed for each swag of 160×100 stitches worked on 10 mesh canvas in cross stitch. (See page 164 for skein lengths of different brands.) If you are making tie-backs, allow an additional 3 hanks of the background colour for each tie-back.

CHARTED COLOURWAY
Key
1	B7	2
2	B6	8
3	B5	11
4	B4	18
5	B3	15
6	B2	11
7	J8	10
8	I7	14
9	J5	19
10	J4	24
11	J6	19
12	I4	23

Background: 4 hanks

ALTERNATIVE COLOURWAY (BRIGHT PINK)
Key
1	A6	2
2	A5	8
3	A4	11
4	A3	18
5	A2	15
6	B2	11
13	J8	10
14	I7	14
15	J5	19
16	J4	24
17	J6	19
18	I4	23

Background: 4 hanks

ALTERNATIVE COLOURWAY 2 (YELLOW)
Key
1	C4	2
2	C3	8
3	C2	11
4	D2	18
5	C1	15
6	D1	11
19	J8	10
20	I7	14
21	J5	19
22	J4	24
23	J6	19
24	I4	23

Background: 4 hanks

SPRING

Spring is my favourite pattern from the Victorian Flowers series of kits which are based on the four seasons of the year. Baskets filled with flowers are perhaps the most frequently used of all motifs worked in embroidery throughout the seventeenth, eighteenth and nineteenth centuries. They are extremely decorative designs whatever form of embroidery has been used and originals are highly collectable.

Although there are many different flowers to

The Rose Swag chart has been specially designed so that it may be easily adapted for use as tie-backs or for pelmets. The key to the outlines is:
25 Pelmet
26 Tie-back

choose from, certain species appear over and over again in embroidered needlework baskets and on the paintings and prints which inspired them. Roses and auriculas appear in practically every example, while tulips, pansies, violets and convolvulous are less popular and many others, such as wall flowers and camellias only occur occasionally.

For my Spring design I chose a mixture of traditional cottage garden flowers that are also needle-workers' favourites. I didn't use roses as they don't flower in spring, but auriculas are there with a primrose, violets, wallflowers, narcissi, bluebells, some rather purple forget me nots and two parrot tulips.

The apple blossom and the nest filled with blue speckled eggs in the foreground emphasize the seasonal nature of the design.

The Spring flower photograph was a pleasure to arrange. Although it was December, we managed to get an incredible variety of spring flowers and these were arranged in various baskets against a small needlework carpet used as a wall hanging. The out sized eggs are painted chicken's eggs in an old deserted blackbird's nest and the lady in the Stafford-shire figure holds a complementary nest of blue speckled eggs in her hands.

As you can see, Spring makes a handsome piece

(Opposite) Woolwork has many uses in a house apart from the obvious cushions and pictures. Pelmets and tie-backs are two that are often overlooked. These swags of roses would help to embellish any room.

(Left and overleaf) A basket filled with spring flowers is a classic embroidery motif. The nest of speckled eggs completes the picture. Spring is one of four designs making up the Four Seasons flower series. It is shown here as part of a carpet, as a framed picture and as the top of a footstool.

Here, the Posy of Violets look wonderfully rich set against the crisp linen sheets and antique fabrics. The three worked examples show the flowers worked on black, cream and brocade patterned backgrounds. Two of the Gothic edgings on the chart have been used as surrounds.

whether part of a carpet, a picture or mounted on the top of a stool. All these examples have been worked on a cream background but black, pale blue, soft rusty red or peach make very pretty alternatives. This is a lovely design to work on through the winter as the cold dark months can be spent sewing in anticipation of gardening pleasures to come.

SPRING
YARN COLOURS AND QUANTITIES

The quantities are the number of yards of Elizabeth Bradley wool needed for each square of 160×160 stitches worked on 10 mesh canvas in cross stitch. (See page 164 for skein lengths of different brands.)

Key		
1	E12	23
2	E9	21
3	E5	32
4	A10	22
5	E2	42
6	N4	14
7	N3	14
8	N1	19
9	K1	7
10	L2	11
11	A7	9
12	B7	19
13	B5	21
14	C5	14
15	D4	21
16	D2	26
17	C1	21
18	F3	6
19	B3	14
20	J8	22
21	I8	31
22	J5	22
23	I2	16
24	I1	10

Background: 6 hanks

A POSY OF VIOLETS

I have found Violets, April hath come on
and the cool winds feel softer, and the rain
Falls in the beaded drops of summer time
For him they flowered
.... with such a simple loveliness among

The common herbs of pasture and breathe out
Their lives so unobtrusively, like hearts
Whose beatings are too gentle for this world.
                    The Victorian Poet – Willis

Violets are a lovely, simple flower, exquisite in colour and symbolize humility. This posy of violets comes from a Victorian cushion I have had for many years and the flowers can be used alone or combined with one of the three patterns shown for a Gothic surround. These Gothic arches are taken from a pattern numbered 1465, which was produced by the famous Berlin woolwork pattern maker, LW Wittich. The chart was lent to me by David Lord Lawrence from a collection of Berlin woolwork charts, and it is a rare and interesting example of this patternmaker's art.

The early nineteenth-century craze for the Gothic style was widespread throughout Europe and prompted the painting and printing of many such charts. I have never seen this particular one used in a piece of Victorian needlework but other similar examples were often worked as borders for a posy of roses or mixed flowers. They have a robust and decorative quality which make them suitable to be used with many twentieth-century fabrics, especially those featuring lattice work or Victorian-style flowers.

I used two of the three borders in the pieces that were made for this book. Both feature the posy of violets as a centrepiece: one was worked against a black background and the other is set against cream. Pale blue, peach or bright pink would be attractive alternatives. The purple shades of the violets are effective with many background colours.

The third piece in the photograph has no Gothic surround. Instead, the violets are framed by a background worked to resemble a piece of brocade. Two shades of cream mimic the dull and shiny parts of the patterned fabric. Stripes, spots or some of the patterned backgrounds shown later in the book (pages 78–87) could be used in the same way.

A whole range of charming pieces can be made using this pattern, apart from the picture and cushions shown. Different backgrounds and combinations could be tried. The Rosebud Wreath, for example (page 53), would make an attractive alternative as a centrepiece, and the Posy of Violets could be framed by the Rose and Primula Border (page 116).

A POSY OF VIOLETS
YARN COLOURS AND QUANTITIES

The quantities are the number of yards of Elizabeth Bradley wool needed for each square of 160×160 stitches worked on 10 mesh canvas in cross stitch. (See page 164 for skein lengths of different brands.) For the background of each: 6 hanks are needed

VIOLETS AND DIAMOND CENTREPIECE
Key

1	M11	20
2	N11	20
3	N10	13
4	N9	11
5	K6	11
6	J8	9
7	J5	13
8	J3	9
9	I9	10
10	J6	8
11	I4	5
12	F8	90
13	F7	45
14	E2	90
15	F6	65
16	C5	2
17	D2	2

VIOLETS AND CIRCULAR CENTREPIECE
(This design makes a square of 166×166 stitches)
Key

1	M11	20
2	N11	20
3	N10	13
4	N9	11
5	K6	11
6	J8	9
7	J5	13
8	J3	9
9	I9	10
10	J6	8
11	I4	5
12	F8	70
13	F7	46
14	E2	58
15	F6	62
16	C5	2
17	D2	2

The Posy of Violets with a Gothic border set against this black background makes a dramatic finished piece of woolwork.

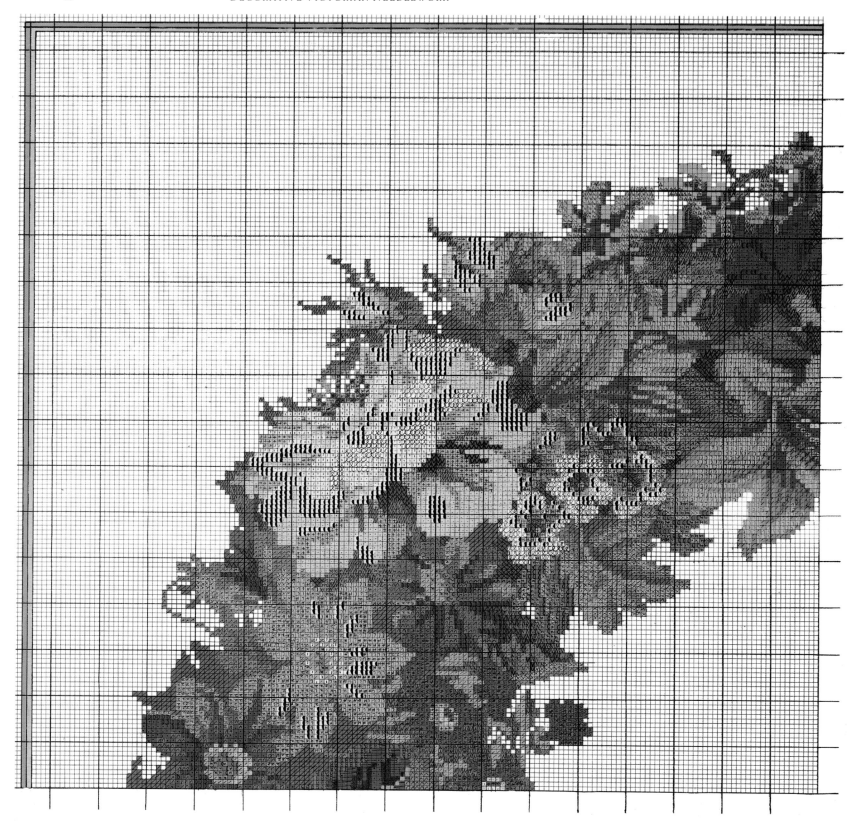

1 2 3 4 5 6 7 8 9 10 11 12 13 14 15

16 17 18 19 20 21 22 23 24 25 26 27 28 29 30 31 32 33 34 35 36 37 38

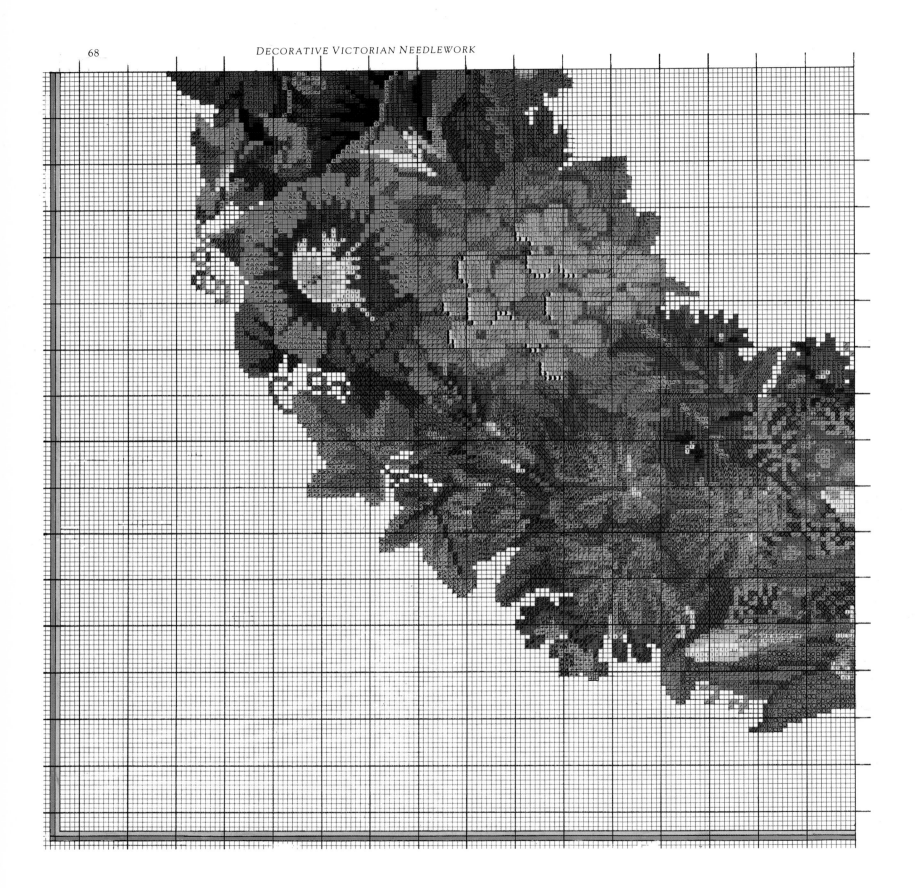

1 2 3 4 5 6 7 8 9 10 11 12 13 14 15

16 17 18 19 20 21 22 23 24 25 26 27 28 29 31 32 35 36 37 38

This giant wreath of flowers makes a splendid project for an ambitious and flower-loving needleperson. It is not really difficult, just big, and I hope you will agree that the result is well worth the effort.

A GIANT WREATH OF FLOWERS

This was the last design that I painted for the book. I was pleased with the designs I had already completed as I felt they made a nicely balanced collection, being a mixture of pretty flowers, chic and amusing animals and some useful repeating patterns and borders grouped together. Even so I was not quite satisfied. I wanted one large and really impressive chart that would be a contrast to the others and a challenge for all those dedicated woolworkers that I know exist.

This giant wreath of flowers is the result. It was a great pleasure to paint as being so large it could include some favourite flowers that I had not had room for in my previous designs. I tried to be reasonably restrained with the number of different colours that I used but even so there are 38 different shades of wool. I could have used many more and I hope you will if you feel it is necessary.

The chart had to be divided into four quarters so that the scale would be large enough to follow when printed in the book – the whole wreath on one page would have made each square impossibly small. The key has been inserted on each half of the printed design (see pages 66–7 and 68–9) for ease of reference. Although the chart is in four sections it is best to work the wreath on one large piece of canvas which can be bought in various widths. (A 36-inch [1-metre] square piece of 10 mesh canvas would be needed to make this design. It allows for a 2-in [5-cm] margin around the design.) Work the flowers first because the wreath plus its background will make the canvas bulky to hold. The more easily worked background can be sewn later with the canvas rolled up and resting on the knees.

When complete, the square can be used as the top of an ottoman or large stool, or it could be hung on a wall or laid on the floor as a small rug. The size of such a rug could be increased by the addition of a border (see page 154 for details about rug making). Black, cream or pale blue would be the most suitable background colours for such rugs as the flowers would show up well against them. For the square on its own a background sewn in wide stripes made from two shades of one colour would be very smart. The bands could be as much as 2 ins (5 cms) wide or even more.

A GIANT WREATH YARN COLOURS AND QUANTITIES

The quantities are the number of yards of Elizabeth Bradley wool needed for each square of 332×332 stitches worked on 10 mesh canvas in cross stitch. (See page 164 for skein lengths of different brands.)

Key		
1	H5	37
2	I11	31
3	I8	31
4	J9	40
5	K10	43
6	K5	68
7	I5	35
8	L11	6
9	L10	29
10	L3	26
11	L2	18
12	L1	17
13	N4	32
14	N3	37
15	N1	28
16	A7	63
17	B8	26
18	B6	49
19	A4	21
20	A3	50
21	B4	40
22	A2	54
23	B2	22
24	C11	22
25	E6	23
26	G6	8
27	G5	8
28	E5	18
29	A10	15
30	E2	30
31	C5	44
32	C3	46
33	D4	14
34	D2	26
35	C1	32
36	J6	63
37	I4	51
38	J8	41
Edging:	C6	27
	I10	27

Background: 28 hanks

CHAPTER THREE

PATTERNED BACKGROUNDS AND GEOMETRIC DESIGNS

(Previous page) Use of colour is just as vital in embroidery as it is in painting. The two early ley figures and the array of paint and brushes emphasize its importance in geometric designs. Gather your palette of wools together before starting to stitch to make sure the colours look good together.

The background is an intrinsic part of a piece of canvas work. It can enhance and complement the main design or, if badly chosen, it can detract from it. It is not always necessary to work a background, however, for if the material on which the piece is being worked is attractive in its own right it can be left uncovered. Indeed, most samplers and much of the needlework done in the Arts and Crafts period were designed to be worked in this way.

Different periods of history favoured characteristic ranges of background colours for woolwork. Sparse, elegant, Regency interiors called for shades of cream, straw or pale blue silk and wool. Tan, coral and cinnamon were also popular colours. Room schemes from this period, though always delicate, were not necessarily pastel in their mood. Later in the nineteenth century, decorating colours became richer and heavier and black, crimson, rust or royal blue were the most common background colours for Berlin woolwork by the 1850s.

As the century progressed, rooms became more and more crowded and furnishings increasingly ornate. Geometric and repeating woolwork designs added to the effect caused by intricately patterned tiles and brickwork. Chairs became heavily carved and sofas were overstuffed and overtrimmed; whole pieces of needlework were often completely covered with pattern. Stained glass windows and molded ceilings all contributed to the aura of rich and textured colours.

Today, most finished needlework pieces seem destined to become cushions. Generally, these are square in shape and the designs worked on them fall into two main styles – either a complete pattern designed for a specific square or a central motif surrounded by an area of background.

In the first style, the square is totally filled by the design. The central concept of the piece is usually framed by an ornate and matching border. In many of the mid-Victorian designs of this type an intricate arrangement of scrolls or leaves surrounds a posy of flowers. Sometimes the flower theme is repeated in a different form in the border. A typical example is the Posy of Violets (page 64) which can be worked with any one of the three Gothic borders included on the chart. In one of them, the purples and greens of the flowers are echoed by the same colours in amongst the Gothic arches.

Alternatively, the square can be completely filled by a picture worked in stitches. Copies of old master paintings, landscapes and thatched cottages are all perennial favourites of this genre. The Rabbits hidden among wild flowers and leaves (page 28) is a new variation on this theme.

Although these sorts of designs are fun to work, the size of the finished piece is limited by the parameters of the pattern. It is difficult to make the square bigger or smaller without considerable skill and experience. This sort of limitation can be circumnavigated by using the second style of designs which consist of a central motif surrounded by an area of simple background.

The central design could be an animal or an arrangement of flowers. Alternatively, it could be something simpler like a set of initials, a family crest or a coat of arms. The final shape and size of the piece can be varied by altering the extent of the background so that it will cover a specific chair, stool or firescreen. It is important, however, that some care is taken to achieve a certain balance between the central picture and the background. A chair seat featuring a tiny flower surrounded by a sea of background would look odd, for example, and in this case a larger design would be more appropriate. Similarly, a fender stool would require a long pattern or the use of a repeating border design, and a round footstool would need a circular motif.

Many Berlin woolwork patterns fall into this second style of patterns. Victorian ladies liked to make a bewildering variety of objects in needlework and the hand-painted Berlin charts were so expensive that they had to be capable of adaptation to as many uses as possible. Border designs and corner motifs were sometimes added to extend the range of a basic pattern; and beadwork, silk stitches or plushwork were used to highlight certain parts of each project. Variations of this type helped to alleviate the tedium of using the same pattern several times over.

The background of a piece of needlework is normally plain, covered by rows of simple stitches worked in a single colour of wool. Basketweave, cross stitch or tent stitch are the three most commonly used stitches and the wool colour can be chosen to match or complement the colour scheme of the room for which the needlework piece is intended. In a period house, a more authentic antique finish is sometimes required, and the wool needs to look as if it has faded unevenly over the years. This effect can be achieved by using two lengths of crewel wool, of slightly different shades, in the needle together rather than a single strand of 4-ply wool. An authentic, faded, black, can be achieved by using a mixture of dark olive green and dark brown wools together.

Another technique for adding interest to large areas of plain background is to work them in a more elaborate stitch while the main design is still sewn in cross or tent stitch. I have occasionally seen a Victorian piece on which this has been done and it looks very effective. A simple geometric stitch is best. Mosaic is quick and easy to work, and Florentine, Gobelin, or brick stitch will cover the canvas quickly. These stitches all produce interesting textures and clear diagrams of them are given on page 147.

As an alternative, the background of a piece can be completely covered with a pattern. Many such small repeating patterns can be seen on the long samplers produced by adults from about 1850 to 1880. These long strips of canvas were a few inches wide and could be up to three or four feet in length. Their edges were neatly bound in coloured silk and they were covered in a random arrangement of tiny designs and patterns worked in many different varieties of stitch. They could be bought already finished from Berlin woolwork emporia to act as pattern guides, or they could be stitched at home as a personal record of designs which could be added to whenever a new variation was discovered. They were worked in the rather extraordinary mixtures of colours favoured by Victorian ladies, and since they were generally not intended for display they were kept rolled up in the workbox, where their colours remained very fresh and unfaded. The mixtures of magenta, lime green, pillar box red and sulphur yellow in all their original undimmed brilliance look somewhat bizarre to our eyes.

Occasionally, large collections of small pieces of canvas covered in tiny samples of work come on the market. These are thought to have belonged to needlework teachers who made them for their pupils to copy. Needlework played a major part in the curriculum of most girls' schools and learning to follow a Berlin pattern in brightly coloured wools was probably a welcome relief from working rows of alphabet or initials in black or red cotton. Most household linen in the nineteenth century was marked with these neat cross stitch letters.

If you have access to a long sampler or a teaching collection then it would be interesting to try some of the patterns found on them, either using the original colours or a selection of your own choice. Most of the geometric charts in this book are based on material from such sources or from the many Berlin patterns featuring such designs that were produced between 1850 and 1880. Some are very complex, and create clever optical effects with their shading and intricate repetitions of the same shapes while others are much simpler. The popularity of Greek and Roman artifacts and architecture early in the century produced a wave of classical motifs which were incorporated into geometric patterns, whereas the later Victorian passion for all things Medieval led to endless Gothic arches, fleur-de-lis and repeating tile designs. Other patterns show folded ribbons, trellis work or simple stars or hexagons intermingled with great imagination and variety. Like all Berlin patterns, the earlier examples tend to be more attractive and are more useful today because they are lighter and more imaginative. Later, the Gothic style became more dominant and the various typical motifs such as arches, trefoils and lancets were often coloured yellow ochre, olive green or brown and outlined in black. These rather ponderous patterns are understandably difficult to use in today's lighter and brighter interiors.

A number of repeating geometric patterns are featured in this book. They range in complexity from simple spots or stripes to quite complicated trellis or interlocking hexagon designs. Even the most complex ones can be used for backgrounds as long as the central motif is kept simple. Initials, a commemorative message or birthday greetings can be set into a simple heart, oval or circular shaped panel and then this can be framed by an area of geometric pattern. Pieces of different shapes and sizes can be made in this way and when complete fashioned into all manner of little objects to be given away or used.

Victorian households must have been busy places in the months before Christmas. Most presents were made by hand and Berlin woolwork items were very popular gifts. Some of the objects, such as pen wipers, hair tidies, face screens, foot muffs or sovereign purses, would not be of much use today. However, other items are well worth making – spectacle or sunglass cases, evening purses and cheque-

This richly coloured piece of woolwork was made in about 1860. Victorian ladies seemed to enjoy embroidering foxes' heads and this one is set against an interesting patterned background worked in six shades of pink and red. The chart I derived from this original piece is called Interlocking Diamonds and Stars and is seen on page 78. The chart is shown here on its side, it doesn't really matter which way round it is worked.

book covers look very smart made in patterned woolwork; slippers, braces, belts and even smoking caps can make unusual fashion accessories; pin cushions, book marks and wedding pillows can be charming, and every dog should have a cross stitch collar for special occasions. Woolwork is strong and hard wearing and such pieces are reasonably easy to construct. If necessary, they should be stiffened with cardboard or buckram, then lined with silk and edged with matching silk bias binding or strips of leather. If a needlework item becomes grubby, it can easily be cleaned with upholstery foam or a liquid carpet cleaner (see page 156).

As a general principle, where the central design of a piece of needlework is elaborate, the background should be plain or feature a relatively simple pattern. The picture should stand out from its background and not be overwhelmed by it. The woolwork featured above is a good example. This original piece of cross stitch embroidery shows a fox holding a duck in its mouth. The fox has been worked against a patterned background which rather resembles patchwork with the diamond shapes stitched in shades of crimson, red and pink. The piece was probably made in about 1860. Although one might expect the rusty brown of the fox's fur to clash horribly with the reds of the background, it does not. The picture works well as a balanced and complete composition with the background pattern adding a richness as well as interest to the central picture. Since the needlework has never been used or framed, it has not been exposed to light and as a result the colours are as bright as on the day it was finished.

I am particularly fond of striped and spotted backgrounds, especially if they are worked in just two colours or two shades of the same colour wool. Spots seem to make a piece look softer and prettier. The Rosebud Wreath featured on page 53 is a very feminine design made even more so by the little dots scattered about on the background. I have not tried working this design with a narrow striped background but since stripes normally add distinction to a piece I would expect them to make it look smarter and more suited to the drawing room than to the bedroom. To be unobtrusive, stripes need to be worked in close shades of one colour wool. If two different colours, such as dark red and bottle green, or red and french blue, are used, the whole effect is much more dramatic and bold. Like a boldly striped blazer, such a background can be very smart when used in the right place. To achieve a smooth finish, stripes need to be worked along their length rather than across, so if the stripes are to run vertically on the finished needlework the whole piece must be worked on its side. The Palamino Horse set against a background worked in two shades of duck egg blue (page 36) was sewn in this way.

Most of the background patterns and geometric designs shown in this book are included in this chapter, but a few more are scattered about in other parts, used as background designs. They can all be worked in any suitable mixture of colours. Some of them, like the repeating leaf pattern on page 89, are marvellous for using up all the odd bits of wool left over from completed kits and other projects. It is a good idea when working geometric designs to gather together all the shades of wool that might suit a particular pattern. A pleasing combination of colours can then be assembled and any clashing hues removed. All the colours used in a room scheme could be combined in one piece. Mixes of pastel colours can be just as effective as the bright shades so beloved of Victorian needlewomen. Totally individual pieces can be made using this sort of pattern and I hope that you find them as interesting and as adaptable as I do.

INTERLOCKING DIAMONDS AND STARS

This design is based on the original piece of Victorian woolwork shown opposite which was probably made in about 1860. The original shows a well resolved fox's head clasping a duck in its mouth and the design is completed with a swag of oak leaves and acorns and a geometric background worked in six shades of pink, red and maroon. I was tempted to reproduce the whole design but I couldn't quite bring myself to chart the poor dead duck. Those of you who like the design and are not quite so squeamish could probably work it from the photograph of the finished piece opposite – the colours are so clear and distinct.

This panel of needlework has never been framed and so the colours are unfaded and are as bright as when the piece was first completed over a hundred years ago. The background is unusual and is made up of a pattern of interlocking diamonds and stars. It is simple and yet most effective. The chart shows the design painted in colours similar to those on the original piece. To produce a blue or green version, just use six shades of these colours instead.

Patterned backgrounds are great fun to try, especially if you find plain ones boring to work. This one would look interesting behind such relatively simple designs as The Palamino Horse (page 33) or The Tabby Cat (page 39). It would also look particularly splendid as a base for a formal family coat of arms or crest particularly if worked in pale colours to provide a contrast to the centrepiece.

With some thought and imagination I am sure you will be able to think of many such combinations using the various patterns in the book. Treat the designs like old-fashioned chidren's building blocks – some are pictorial while others are plain and they can be put together in an endless variety of ways.

INTERLOCKING DIAMONDS AND STARS
YARN COLOURS AND QUANTITIES

The quantities are the number of yards of Elizabeth Bradley wool needed for each area of 50×20 stitches (or any other 10sq in [25sq cm] combination) worked on 10 mesh canvas in cross stitch. (See page 164 for skein lengths of different brands.)

(Right) The chart for Interlocking Diamonds and Stars.

(Opposite) Six simple background designs which can be used singly or in combination to add variety to many of the designs in this book. The colour keys are provided so that you can see exactly how many colours are used for each design.

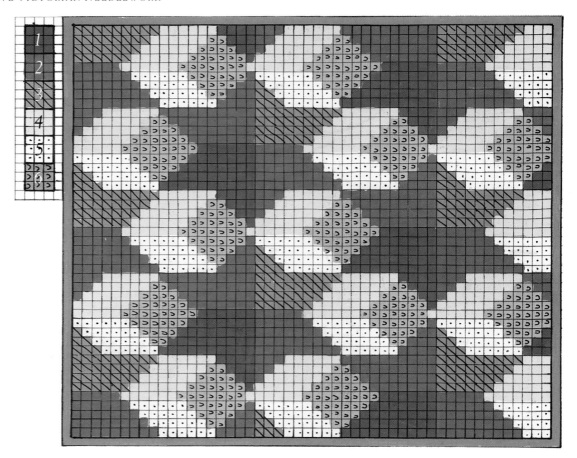

Key		
1	A7	3
2	B8	6
3	B7	3
4	B6	3
5	B4	4
6	B3	3

SIX SMALL BACKGROUND CHARTS

Stripes are a very simple form of patterned background and these six little charts show some variations on the basic theme. Charts One and Two show vertical stripes worked in two shades of blue wool. In the first, alternate rows are worked in each colour to create a restrained and almost textured effect. A bolder pin-stripe would be achieved by using two different colours – dark green and cream, or pink and white, would both be effective.

In Chart Two, the stripes are wider and each is made up of four rows of stitches. The Palamino Horse has a background worked in this way (see photograph on page 36) and it adds interest to the basic pictorial design. For a really large piece such as the Giant Wreath of Flowers (see charts on pages 66–69), bolder, even wider, stripes of six or seven rows are a possibility. Sewn in two shades of cream they would add to the decorative quality of the finished square.

Charts Three and Four show further elaboration upon a basic stripe. On Chart Three, cream stripes, each three rows wide, have been interspaced between the two-tone blue ones. The same configuration, but with a different mixture of colours, is shown on page 29 as a background to a spaniel firescreen. As the pattern of stripes becomes more elaborate it ceases to be merely a backdrop and becomes on integral part of the whole design. Some care should be taken choosing the colours, for clashing

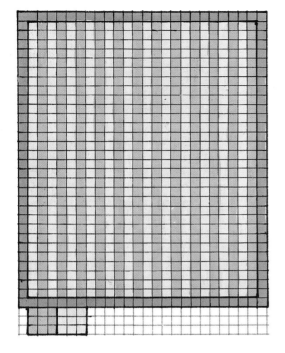

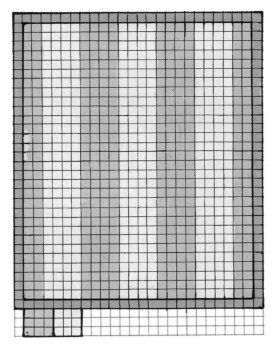

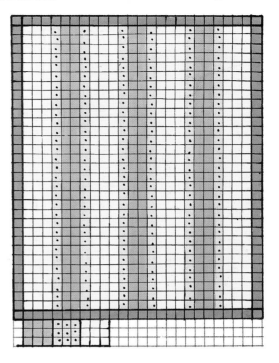

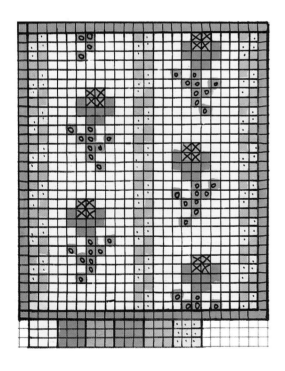

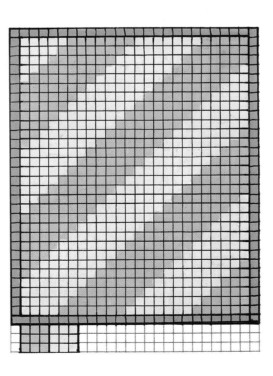

Here the background designs are shown worked. The finished effect can be clearly seen.

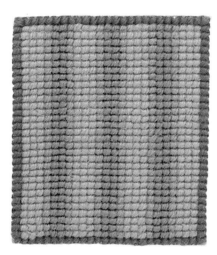

shades or too bright a mixture can overwhelm and detract from the centre design. One colour affects the look of another when they are put next to each other and it is therefore best to work a small, sample section before deciding on the final mixture that will be used.

Chart Four shows an even more complicated vertically striped design. Tiny green and pink rosebuds have been added to each cream band while the blue lines have been broken up so that they resemble a length of thin cord. A striped design with this degree of pattern is more difficult to use than a simpler one. This one is best used alone or as an integral part of a needlework picture. Dash the Spaniel (page 30) would look charming set against such a background – it would look as if the little dog was standing against a prettily papered bedroom wall.

When working all of these patterns, the rows of stitches should progress along the stripes rather than across them. This means that the whole piece will need to be worked on its side for the stripes to run vertically on the finished item.

The last two patterns show diagonal stripes and

these charts may prove interesting for those needle-workers who like to use basketweave stitch to cover their background areas (see page 145) instead of cross stitch. Basketweave stitch is sewn diagonally across the canvas and if worked in stripes would be both smart to look at and less tedious to sew. Charts Five and Six both show two-tone blue stripes, seven stitches wide. On Chart Five the bands of colour are plain, whereas on Chart Six small motifs have been added at regular intervals to make a more elaborate background covering.

Striped backgrounds are so decorative and yet they are very rarely used; perhaps next time you have a large area of background to cover it would be worth considering one of them.

INTERLOCKING HEXAGONS

This design is constructed from all sorts of geometric shapes that combine to make a pattern of interlocking hexagons. It is taken from an old needlework cushion that I bought during my travels around antique shops and it is a useful design for many pur-

The soft pinks, greens and yellows used for these Interlocking Hexagons (see chart overleaf) make a pretty piece when mixed together.

poses and in many different situations.

First of all, like all the patterns in this chapter, it is infinitely extendable and pieces can be made any shape or size. Successful cushions, chair seats or stool covers can be fashioned by using it, as can larger panels for wall hangings or carpets. A plain band of stitches around the edge of such a piece could make a suitably simple border and the colours chosen could be a mixture of those used to decorate the room into which it will eventually go. The shades could be pastel, bright or muted in tone – it really doesn't matter as long as they complement each other and don't clash. For the design used in this book I used a mixture of pale greens, pinks, yellows and ochres, which are all great favourites of mine. I have a pale lime-green drawing room and the cushion made from the prototype looks good making a nice contrast to the other cushions.

Most Victorian woolwork designs are pictorial, pretty and elaborate: while they look attractive in most styles of room they can appear a little odd in very stark modern interiors. This simpler pattern would suit such a room admirably and look very striking worked in shades of gray and cream or in a range of bright primary colours.

The pattern can be started at any point as it has no definite edge but it looks best if a hexagon is placed in the centre and the others radiate outwards. The chart is easy to follow once a small portion has been mastered and the pattern has enough variety to make it continually interesting to work.

INTERLOCKING HEXAGONS
YARN COLOURS AND QUANTITIES

The quantities are the number of yards of Elizabeth Bradley wool needed for each area of 161×161 stitches worked on 10 mesh canvas in cross stitch. (See page 164 for skein lengths of different brands.)

Key		
1	I8	54
2	I5	104
3	K4	120
4	C3	124
5	C1	40
6	F3	58
7	B4	15
8	B2	93

THREE SMALL GEOMETRIC DESIGNS

Geometric patterns became increasingly popular as the nineteenth century progressed and many small

Divided Diamonds is a comparatively straightforward repeating background design. The chart is overleaf.

Divided Diamonds.

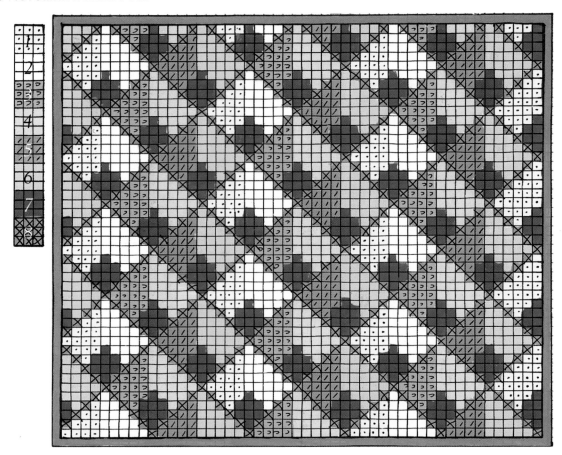

items of woolwork were made from them to be given as presents or sold at charity bazaars. Slippers, purses, bookmarks or spectacle cases are just a few of the more practical examples of such fancy work. Charts for designs like these are generally quite small as only a tiny portion of the ever-repeating pattern needs to be shown. This feature made them popular as free gifts in the ladies' magazines of the period and thus they became widely distributed among the Berlin woolwork sewing public at that time.

The three designs shown here were painted using such small charts as models. They are all variations on a basic diamond shape surrounded by latticework. The simplest of them shows divided diamonds worked in two shades of three colours. Each colour follows the other in a rigid sequence repeated throughout the piece. Every diamond is divided into two halves and a smaller and darker one has been placed in each right hand corner. The trellis is made

from a single line of stitches and it connects and frames each diamond.

In the second, relatively straight forward, chart the latticework is made up of overlapping stripes worked in four shades of pink graduating to rusty red and maroon. The diamond shapes inside the trellis are worked with plain green wool.

The third pattern is the most complicated. Both the trellis and the diamonds framed by it are elaborated with intricate patterns and a total of eight colours has been used for the piece.

Apart from their obvious value as designs for making small gift items, these charts can be used to make covers for stools, as wide surrounding frames for other woolwork or as interesting alternative squares for patchwork cushions or carpets. Any mixture of colours can be tried, to create rich and unusual combinations. The charts should prove to be useful adjuncts to other ideas in this book.

Overlapping Ribbons.

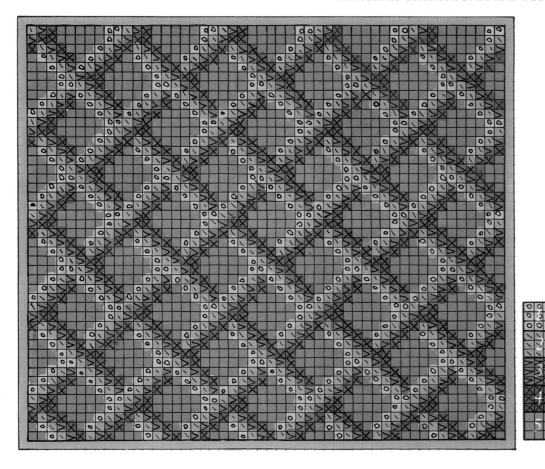

DIVIDED DIAMONDS
YARN COLOURS AND QUANTITIES

The quantities are the number of yards of Elizabeth Bradley wool needed for each area of 50×20 stitches (or any other 10sq in [25sq cm] combination) worked on 10 mesh canvas in cross stitch. (The instructions to the right provide guidance on calculating yarn quantities and see page 164 for skein lengths of different brands.)

Key

1	C3	3
2	C2	3
3	B4	3
4	B2	3
5	K4	3
6	J2	3
7	N4	6
8	N7	6

OVERLAPPING RIBBONS
YARN COLOURS AND QUANTITIES

The quantities are the number of yards of Elizabeth Bradley wool needed for each area of 50×20 stitches (or any other 10sq in [25sq cm] combination) worked on 10 mesh canvas in cross stitch. The border row isn't included. To cover a larger area, work out the finished size of the piece, divide the area by 10 (or by 25 if working in metric) and multiply the yarn quantities given here by the result in order to establish how much yarn is required. (See page 164 for skein lengths of different brands.)

Key

1	B4	5
2	B6	5
3	B8	5
4	A7	5
5	J8	9

ELABORATE OVERLAPPING RIBBONS
YARN COLOURS AND QUANTITIES

The quantities are the number of yards of Elizabeth Bradley wool needed for each area of 50×20 stitches (or any other 10sq in [25sq cm] combination) worked on 10 mesh canvas in cross stitch. The border row isn't included. (See page 164 for skein lengths of different brands.)

Key

1	C1	3
2	B4	3
3	B6	3
4	K4	4
5	J8	6
6	N1	3
7	N6	4
8	M11	5

REPEATING LEAVES

A maple leaf is repeated over and over to form this design. The indentations of the leaves fit cleverly together to make an interlocking patchwork. The pattern is based on another of the original Victorian cushions that I have owned for many years. I am particularly fond of it both from a design and colour

Both this design, the Overlapping Ribbons and the Elaborate Overlapping Ribbons (charted opposite and photographed overleaf) are examples of increasingly complicated patterns. They can, of course, be worked in any mixture of colours.

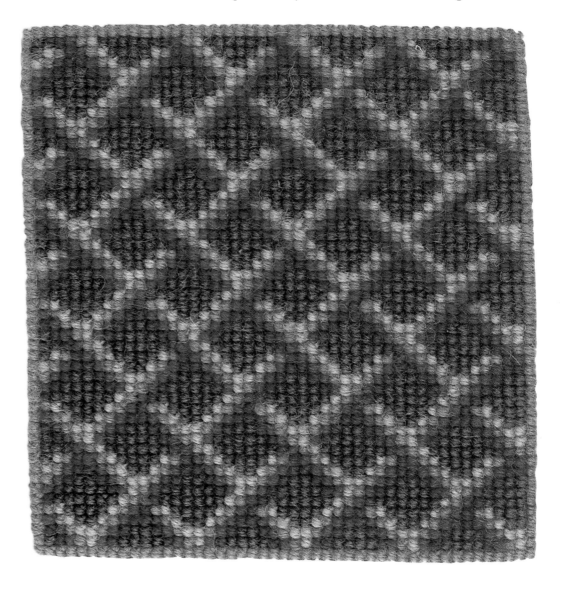

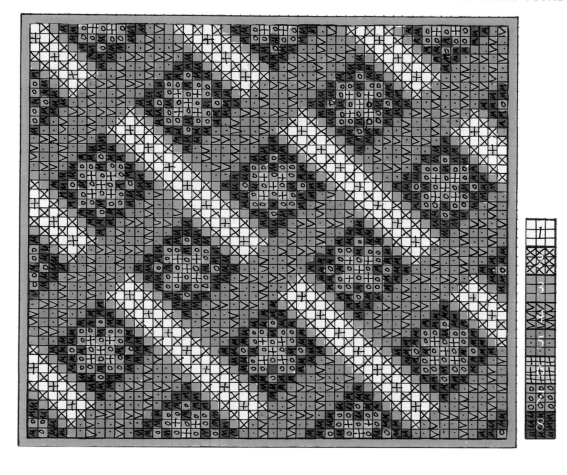

Elaborate overlapping ribbons.

point-of-view and also because it is so very interesting to work.

A different colour could be used for every single leaf on the cushion piece if one wished, although it would mean having over 100 different shades available. Indeed, this is a marvellous pattern for using up odd lengths of wool left over from other projects. Each leaf uses about 2 yards of wool if it is worked in cross stitch on a 10 mesh canvas. This may seem a surprisingly large quantity to cover such a small area but bear in mind that the starting and finishing off necessary at the ends of the longer rows uses more wool than working a single line of stitches.

I found the chart interesting to paint even though the pattern is repetitive. After much trial and error I discovered that I needed a mixture of light, dark, muted and pastel colours all mixed together to make a vibrant whole. This was very similar to the original combination on my Victorian cushion though some

of the wools had become so faded as to be indistinguishable from one another.

I enjoy peculiar mixes of strong colours which is probably one of the reasons I like Berlin woolwork so much. If you don't, then try a rather more pastel mix or a rusty autumnal range of shades. I found the pattern became rather dull if I kept within a narrow group of tones and advise the addition of a few oddly coloured leaves to keep the square lively.

The diamond border is not original and is optional. I felt a border of some sort made a frame for the design rather than having the leaf shapes just peter out over the edge of the piece.

REPEATING LEAVES
YARN COLOURS AND QUANTITIES

The quantities are the number of yards of Elizabeth Bradley wool needed for each square of 159×159

By changing the colours of the Elaborate Overlapping Ribbons design, the pattern can be subtly altered.

(Opposite and overleaf) This design of Repeating Leaves is marvellous for using up odd bits of wool. As you can see, it looks equally decorative made up as a cushion or as a cover for a small Victorian footstool. (The wool quantities are indicated on the right.)

stitches worked on 10 mesh canvas in cross stitch. (See page 164 for skein lengths of different brands.)

Key

1	I10	104	11	N1	45
2	I7	20	12	H2	18
3	J5	19	13	A11	10
4	I4	16	14	A7	15
5	I5	20	15	B8	15
6	J8	14	16	A4	28
7	K4	13	17	A3	19
8	L1	11	18	B2	27
9	C5	19	19	B5	19
10	D9	23	20	A9	23
			21	C1	29
			22	D2	27
			23	C3	17

CHAPTER FOUR

··········

REPEATING PATTERNS

(Previous page) In this picture, the Barley Twists and Cornflowers design (see chart on page 99) is shown worked in the palest colourway. The cushion and country chair have both been covered in the same delicate design worked on a cream background – even I would enjoy ironing in a room like this!

Repeating patterns are designs that can be extended indefinitely and thus can be used for making pieces of needlework of any shape or size. Large panels can be sewn to act as wall hangings or carpets and different sorts of furniture from chaiselongues to small stools can be covered in matching designs. The patterns repeat in the same way as a fabric or a wallpaper and those featured here are of varying complexity, mood and subject. The needlework made from such designs can be used to cover almost any style and size of furniture and will suit most periods of room decoration and interiors.

Many people like to make a piece of needlework for a specific purpose. This could be a cushion square or a cover for a piece of furniture in their house. Stools of various shapes and sizes seem to be popular subjects for refurbishment as do sets of dining chairs both period and new, while many firescreens and old polescreens need new centre pieces. Making a new woolwork covering for any of these objects allows for personal choice and would be a manageable and interesting project.

Most people have at least one stool tucked away somewhere in their house and most of them would be enhanced by a pretty, new needlework cover. Pianos and dressing tables often have matching seats. Using a foot stool when knitting or sewing can help to prevent backache and needlework shops often sell such small pieces to be covered for just this purpose. Thousands of stools of different styles, shapes and sizes were made between about 1830 and 1880. They are not only sturdy little items of furniture but are most attractive and useful. They were usually well constructed and many of them have survived to be collectors' pieces in our houses today. The original fabric or needlework cover is often worn beyond repair; a replacement in keeping with its age and character would be well worth making.

Antique stools have become very fashionable and so the demand for them has grown while the supply of authentic pieces remains limited. Large examples are much sought after and have become expensive; they make practical and attractive coffee tables or spare seats and look marvellous covered in suitable needlework. The art of producing really excellent copies of antique furniture seems to have blossomed over the last ten years. A particularly handsome type of stool has a padded rectangular seat and turned mahoghany or walnut legs each tipped with a brass castor. Copies are available from several manufacturers and some of them will make the rectangular tops in virtually any dimensions that you choose. The legs are generally made in two lengths, one suitable for coffee tables and the other for piano or dressing table stools. Some names and addresses of manufacturers are given on page 159 but the 'new product' and classified sections of the glossy decorating magazines contain others if you want them.

Fashion has also rescued box ottomans from boxrooms and bonfires. These upholstered boxes with hinged lids could at one time be found in most junk shops or sales of household clutter. They are now more likely to be discovered renovated and recovered in smart shops specializing in decorative antiques. Some ottomans are a simple box shape, others have tapering sides like a wine cooler and further elaboration in the form of mahogany mouldings and lion's paw feet adorn more elegant drawing room models. There are also bedroom varieties shaped like chaise longues with padded and buttoned backs and long box seats. Early nineteenth-century ottomans are generally smaller than later ones and their elegant forms are often totally covered by needlework. Others have a needlework top and sides of fabric – ribbed ottoman cloth, velvet, brocade or tammy (a fine woollen fabric) are typical. Again they make excellent coffee tables or spare seats and as storage units for spare wool they are unbeatable.

Versions of some of the more elegant ottomans are reproduced, but many simple late nineteenth- and early twentieth-century models can still be found for a relatively modest cost in antique shops and salerooms. They will probably need a certain amount of refurbishment but they are easy to cover since the sides and top are simple in shape and straightforward to measure. Some sort of picture on top and a geometric pattern on the sides would be traditional. Sometimes the whole piece was covered in the same patterned needlework and a thin cord was sewn round the top and down and round each side. This cord acts as a frame for each of the five sections and also disguises the fact that the pattern does not necessarily join up at each corner. With their love of trimmings and elaborate furnishings, the Victorians sometimes added tassels at each corner for good measure.

Dining chairs almost demand to be covered in

needlework, which is such a soft warm material, and is hardwearing and easily cleaned – almost perfect for its purpose.

Sets of six, eight or twelve dining chairs are often handed down through the generations of a family. Complete or harlequin sets can be bought from antique shops, fairs or sales and good copies of most period styles can now be purchased. To cover such a set of chairs is a major commitment of time and quite an investment in materials. In spite of the rather daunting nature of the task it does seem to be a project that many people would like to tackle. They are understandably nervous about how they might go about it (see page 156 for advice on planning the outline).

Such a project will necessarily take a long time to complete but remember that hopefully the chair seats will still be in use fifty to a hundred years hence. The pattern or design that is chosen should be interesting enough to hold your attention and make the pieces a pleasure to sew even twelve times over if you are lucky enough to have a set of twelve chairs. The colour range chosen could be of generally pastel, rich, muted, or bright shades of wool. Ideally, each seat cover should include at least six to ten colours so that they are as adaptable as possible and would fit into several colour schemes if necessary. You might find that by the time they are all finished, you may have redecorated your dining room two or three times.

I would find it quite impossible to ever complete twelve chair seats all exactly the same. Knowing this before I started, I would therefore make the designs all related in some way but not identical. Twelve small geometric patterns would be smart. The twelve animals from our Victorian Animals series could be stunning on a set of plain chairs. Flowers are always popular and really are very adaptable – the choice is yours.

Without being too precious about it, the needlework pattern used should have some relevance to the style and period of the piece of furniture to be covered. For example, a classic, sabre-legged Regency dining chair would look better covered in some form of striped design or a simple repeating leaf shape than in great bunches of roses and hollyhocks. As a rule, if the piece to be covered has straight simple lines then a restrained pattern or classic design is best. If, on the other hand it has fat turned legs

or carved cabriole legs and rococo curlicues – then fruit, flowers and generally more rampageous designs are a possibility. Most of all, however, it is important to really like the designs that you have chosen. You will then be eager to get started, enjoy working them and actually finish them.

If persuasiveness rather than persistence is a strong character trait, then perhaps a set of chair seats, each completed by a friend or relation might be more practical than trying to make them all yourself. At Claydon House in Buckinghamshire, England, there is a set of upholstered arm chairs covered in Berlin woolwork. Each is stitched with a different repeating pattern and each was worked by a different friend of the family.

Most people tend to like a certain range of colours. I like both pastel and primary colours but for our own house I always seem to end up using muted versions of rich, early autumnal colours mixed with lots of black. I would thus cover my chairs using either a series of geometric patterns worked in a mixture of these colours or combine them in a set of different flowers designs. The various bunches, wreaths and baskets of flowers would all be worked against black backgrounds. I could be pretty sure that the chairs would fit into almost any room in our house as long as I kept within this general range of shades which includes rusts, browns, ochres, soft yellows, purples and mauves, crimson, peach and pink, greeny blues and yellowy greens. If you look around your house carefully and analytically you should be able to tell the range of tints that you tend to use in your decorating schemes. These may be different from the colours that you like in an abstract sense or from favourite colours that you use for your clothes. If you stick to this range then hopefully your chair seats will end up being used rather than ending up in a plastic bag in a saleroom like so many others I have seen over the years.

The nineteenth century is sometimes called The Age of Revivals. In a revival, the fashions and styles of a past historic period are resurrected and refurbished for use in the present time. Throughout the nineteenth century, the various revivals of different period styles rapidly followed each other, though it was not an orderly progression since the trends tended to merge into one another and get mixed up. The whole picture was further complicated by the fact that France, Britain and North America all had

The Barley Twists and Cornflowers design (see chart on page 99) can be stitched in various colourways. Here, the brightest version with a black background is illustrated.

slightly different sets of revivals happening at the same time. Fabrics, furniture and needlework patterns moved between the three countries with the normal movements of trade. This activity was further exaggerated in the nineteenth century by the enormous number of people who moved from crowded Europe to North America throughout the period. The immigrants took their taste, mementos and design traditions with them.

In order to understand the many forms of nineteenth-century furniture, and thus the type of needlework to put on them, it is necessary to look briefly at the many influences at work. Early in the nineteenth century, from about 1800 to 1830, furniture was classical, elegant and, on the whole, reasonably restrained. French influence and Empire

style were strong guiding forces. Fabric rather than needlework was used to cover upholstered furniture with the exception of dining chairs, cushions, bolsters and a few small armchairs. Some very decorative, small, upright chairs with cane seats were made, particularly in America and the seats were often covered by small flat cushions known as chair pads. These were frequently covered in needlework and are generally exceptionally pretty little pieces. The Duchess of York worked coverings for a sofa and a set of armchairs during this period. She devized a pattern of baskets of flowers surrounded by leaves. Cornucopia, baskets and urns of flowers were popular motifs in Britain at this time. The French were fond of lions, bees, arrows, gods and goddesses and the letter N – for Napoleon – usually surrounded by a laurel wreath. In America, eagles, lyres, pine-apples, stars, dolphins and lotus flowers were stitched and these motifs give their needlework its own distinctive flavour.

The revivals really got going in full force after about 1830. A Gothic revival was one of the first and most romantic. Chairbacks, windows and architecture all suddenly featured charming pointed arches; romantic turrets and castellations were added to houses, and ruins, grottos and follies were built in gardens throughout the country.

It was a most decorative period and the simpler painted furniture and artifacts produced are very desirable. A later Gothic revival produced much heavier furniture and architecture. The Gothic surrounds framing the Posy of Violets on page 64 are from an early pattern. Needlework was often used to cover small pieces of furniture — some covers featured Gothic arches, lancets and crockets but on the whole simple flower arrangements, borders of leaves and berries or pictures of idyllic landscapes were more popular. The craze for Berlin woolwork was just beginning to get underway and most of the patterns were still quite small and simple in form. A certain restraint was still in evidence.

The style of furniture that most people associate with the Victorians was Rococo. It was a very popular revival and featured carving, curlicues, scrolls, cabriole legs and balloon back chairs. Furniture makers such as John Belter in America elaborated the basic designs of his chairs with a characteristic carved and upstanding ruff on the back. The carving on the frames of the chairs became gradually heavier and the legs more ponderous as the century progressed. Some late Victorian armchairs had balloon backs and heavy turned legs instead of cabriole ones — a rather unsuccessful combination.

Among the many items of rococo furniture used in the typical Victorian house were pairs of small arm chairs, one slightly smaller than the other. They were very popular and were sometimes known as ladies' and gentlemen's chairs. Generally, they were covered in fabric, made to look more elaborate by deeply buttoning the upholstery. Sometimes, however, a cover was made in Berlin woolwork. Special patterns shaped to fit the seats and backs of such chairs were produced and these were available in most of the more popular types of designs of the day. Flowers seem to have been most frequently used

and the bright, naturalistic bouquets, posies and swags are particularly suited to these charming little chairs. As with stools, modern copies are available and covering one would make a pleasant project. The Wreath of Roses (page 48) or the Repeating Roses (page 103) designs could both be adapted to fit the seat and back sections of a ladies' chair. A narrow striped background would lift the design if extra smartness was required.

In the meantime, from about 1840 to 1860, France was busy with its Louis Quartorze, Quinze and Seize revivals. Britain was enjoying its Medieval and Elizabethan periods with prie-Dieu chairs and massive throne-like dining furniture. Both influences spread to North America some years later to join the Renaissance, New Greek and Colonial revivals already enjoying popularity there.

Until about 1860, roses, landscapes and animals were embroidered on almost anything from cushions, pictures and slippers to covers for stools, chairs and sofas. After that, things got rather out of hand. Generally, patterns declined in quality and different styles became hopelessly mixed. Needlewomen seemed to have become very confused as to what pattern to put on what style of furniture — perhaps they did not care that much as long as it was ornate and fun to work. Gothic arches became entwined with roses; bunches of gloxineas and other hot-house flowers found their way on to Elizabethan ecclesiastical thrones. The more disciplined geometric patterns were extensively used from about 1850 until they too became over simplified and ugly. Thoroughly bewildered, many needlewomen turned thankfully to the new Arts and Craft needlework in the later part of the century. Nevertheless, Berlin woolwork has continued to be made on a modest scale right up to the present day. Its practicality as a covering for furniture is hard to beat.

BARLEY TWISTS AND CORNFLOWERS

The chart for this ornate and delicate repeating pattern has been painted to present three possible colourways of the same design. The photographs show each one worked separately and it is interesting to see how the mood of each piece is totally changed by the range of colours that have been used in it. Moving from left to right across the chart, the first colourway shows a combination of purples, peaches, ochres and burgundy reds. This is an unusual mix of shades especially when set against a duck egg blue background as in the worked example. The mood is mellow and interesting. With a golden, tobacco-brown ground the piece would become even richer and perhaps be suitable for use as a library cushion, to be placed in a worn and comfortable armchair against a rich backdrop of tooled leather books.

The second example (centre) is stitched with wools in bright primary tones against a black background – my favourite combination for it is fresh and cheerful and yet very smart. It looks perfect in my kitchen and would be hard wearing and and practical in such a setting.

The last example (right) is totally different again. The palest pinks, blues and straw yellows are stitched against a background of 'Devon cream' wool. It makes an ideal combination to enhance a pretty pas-

tel bedroom or bathroom. Such light colours would be impractical for the general wear and tear of everyday household use, but a delight in an occasionally occupied guestroom.

The chart itself is made up of a border resembling a string of oval-shaped beads between two lines of stitching. It surrounds a central area in which a series of stripes like twisted sticks of barley sugar run from top to bottom. They are broken at intervals by sprigs of cornflowers and leaves. Each part of the pattern can be used alone, as can be seen on the chair seat on page 93 where only the central portion has been worked. Using the border alone, narrow straps, belts and braces or edgings for other designs can be made.

The pattern can be used in many different ways and an infinite number of colourways are possible. Just look at the colours in your house or in your wool basket and pick out a suitable mix. Survey your chairs or stools and see which might benefit from a new cover. If you have any room left on your sofa and chairs for cushions, then ones like those shown in the photograph on pages 22–23 all make good projects.

Of the three colourways provided on the chart opposite, the stitched version below is that on the left.

CORNFLOWERS
YARN COLOURS AND QUANTITIES

The quantities are the number of yards of Elizabeth Bradley wool needed for each square of 143×143 stitches worked on 10 mesh canvas in cross stitch. (See page 164 for skein lengths of different brands.)

COLOURWAY 1 (LEFT)
Key

1	A7	20
2	B8	50
3	B5	32
4	N4	9
5	N7	50
6	N5	17
7	I8	22
8	I4	32
9	E4	13
10	E1	7

Background: 6 hanks

Colourways 2 and 3 are shown on page 100.

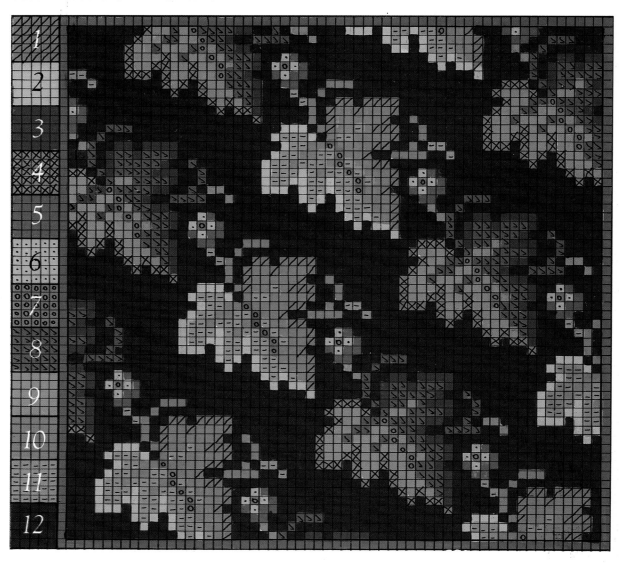

COLOURWAY 2 (CENTRE)

Key

11	L11	20
12	L10	50
13	L3	32
14	A6	9
15	B7	50
16	B5	17
17	J8	22
18	J6	32
19	D4	7
20	C2	13

Background: 6 hanks

COLOURWAY 3 (RIGHT)

Key

21	L3	20
22	L1	50
23	K1	32
24	A3	9
25	A2	50
26	B1	17
27	K4	22
28	J2	32
29	C2	7
30	F3	13

Background: 6 hanks

LEAVES AND BERRIES

There was a fashion for small, restrained, repeating patterns early in the nineteenth century. During the short reign of William IV, furniture and fabric styles were mid-way between the elegance of the Regency and the Rococo curliness of the Victorian period. The library furniture made at this time was particularly fine and the handsome desks and bookcases and the splendid solid library chairs are often used as models for much of the reproduction office furniture made today. Most of the later Berlin patterns are really too pretty to suit such masculine pieces whereas small repeating motifs worked on dark backgrounds complement them perfectly.

The ordered arrangement of leaves and berries shown on this chart is a typical example of such a pattern. The original model for the design was lent to me by Miss Pamela Quail and the worked square is stitched in the same colours as those suggested including the background. Dark blue, brown or a deep wine red would make attractive alternatives.

Such a pattern is not really suitable for large items such as carpets or wall hangings, since the motif is too small to be effective at a distance. It does, however, make up into splendid coverings for desk chairs, stools or small formal cushions.

LEAVES AND BERRIES
YARN COLOURS AND QUANTITIES

The quantities are the number of yards of Elizabeth Bradley wool needed for each square of 160×160 stitches worked on 10 mesh canvas in cross stitch. (See page 164 for skein lengths of different brands.)

Key		
1	N7	37
2	N5	37
3	N4	37
4	N1	37
5	A6	45
6	A4	14
7	G5	24
8	I10	56
9	I7	37
10	J6	56
11	I4	37
12	G11	7 hanks

When stitched, the Leaves and Berries design looks far more complex than it actually is.

REPEATING ROSES

I suspect that this pattern will be one of the most frequently used of all those that I painted for this book as it epitomizes the charm that so many Berlin woolwork patterns offer. The design is based on a large unfinished piece of woolwork that I bought many years ago and the flowers are typically well-resolved and realistic representations of roses and open hollyhock flowers with their buds and leaves.

I have seen several examples of similar patterns since then and in each the flowers are worked in slightly different colours. I decided to use a mixture of soft pastel shades for the flowers on my chart as such colours are pretty and appealling. If you would prefer brighter blooms, it is easy to substitute more vivid tones. Gradually darkening ranges of cherry reds and crimsons or golden yellows could be used, and creams and whites or peach mixed with a soft orange are other possible options.

The flowers are arranged on the chart so that the areas of background are pleasantly interspersed among the flowers. Each group is connected to the next diagonally across the piece and the colours of each pair of hollyhocks and roses change round as the pattern proceeds vertically. The pink and yellow flowers alternate with the rust and buff versions across the chart. If desired, each flower could be worked in a different basic colour and the multi-colour blooms so created could be combined in a much more random arrangement than I have shown. The design leaves plenty of scope for imagination and individual preference.

Any size or shape of piece can be constructed. A large square or oblong carpet worked in the pattern could be most decorative, particularly if framed with the Tassel Border shown on page 121. A simple striped band would make an extremely pleasant alternative margin, and its colours could echo those of the flowers.

Many background colours are possible. I chose black and cream for the pieces made up here – cream gives a very pretty and delicate effect as can be seen in the photograph below. A black background is very dramatic and is more hardwearing as it shows the dust and dirt far less than a paler colour. The chair

opposite has been much improved by its new and very splendid cover. Ottomans, dining chairs or stools would all respond well to similar treatment.

REPEATING ROSES
YARN COLOURS AND QUANTITIES

The quantities are the number of yards of Elizabeth Bradley wool needed for each square of 160×160 stitches worked on 10 mesh canvas in cross stitch. (See page 164 for skein lengths of different brands.)

Key		
1	B8	5
2	B7	14
3	B5	43
4	B4	21
5	A4	6
6	A3	14
7	A2	26
8	B2	18
9	A10	5
10	E3	20
11	E1	41
12	F5	30
13	C5	4
14	C3	6
15	C2	24
16	C1	15
17	D10	7
18	D9	21
19	I3	29
20	J2	41
21	K5	14
22	K3	29
23	K2	29
24	J5	40
25	I5	35

Background: 5 hanks

PAISLEY

Paisley shawls were very much a part of every fashionable woman's wardrobe from the middle of the eighteenth century until the advent of the bustle

(Opposite) The beauty of repeating patterns is that they can be used to make needlework pieces of any size or shape, including the odd shapes needed for upholstering furniture. This desk chair certainly looks very dramatic in its new cover of roses against a black background.

(Overleaf) Paisley shawls and fabrics are once more very fashionable. With this pattern (also featured to the left), you can embroider cushions, and chair or stool covers to match.

More foxes' heads, but this time they are tiny ones complete with silk whiskers that can be used to make many small needlework items. The picture shows a pair of foxy slippers and a waistcoat worked against the traditional dark blue background.

some one hundred years later. Originally, they came from Kashmir but they were soon copied by British manufacturers in Paisley and Norwich. The shawls are large pieces of finely woven wool, fringed at both ends and covered in intricate and stylized patterns. Their most characteristic colours are shades of brick red and orange with small amounts of black and cream. These shawls are exquisite examples of the weaver's art, tough, hardwearing and most attractive from a visual point of view. Their only enemies are moths, and interior decorators who like to cut them up to make chair covers.

As nineteenth-century pattern makers copied every sort of fabric from lace to brocade it is not surprising to find that they attempted to copy Paisley patterns as well. On the whole they were not very successful and although I have several early charts showing Paisley designs, I have never yet seen a worked example. The chart given here is unusual. It is a Paisley-type pattern rather than an exact shawl design but as I hope you will agree it is both stylish and decorative. The original Victorian chart from which the design was taken again belongs to David Lord Lawrence. It is the only example of this particular pattern that I have seen although I own several similar ones all painted on either black or dark blue backgrounds. I have kept some of the rusty colours from the original chart but changed others as many of the shades were very strident. It must be remembered that the Victorian woolwork that we like so much today is a pale and muted version of the vividly brilliant and garish pieces made in the nineteenth century. Magenta is a very fine colour, but used to excess and combined with sulphur yellow, lime green and orange it can become difficult to place.

This design can be quite exacting to work as the pattern meanders all over the place and it is easy to make mistakes. The design does look marvellous when it is worked correctly, however. The photograph shows Paisley woolwork set among a whole mass of Paisley shawls like those that inspired the original chart.

PAISLEY
YARN COLOURS AND QUANTITIES

The quantities are the number of yards of Elizabeth Bradley wool needed for each repeat of 60×85 stitches worked on 10 mesh canvas in cross stitch.

(See page 164 for skein lengths of different brands.)

Key

1	L5	2
2	L4	2
3	L3	2
4	K5	2
5	J5	4
6	I5	4
7	N4	1
8	N1	1
9	N7	1
10	N5	1
11	C11	6
12	E12	5
13	E7	9
14	B4	1
15	C6	8
16	D4	4
17	D2	3
18	G4	1
19	G2	3
20	F5	3
21	F3	3
22	C3	8

Background: 1–2 hanks

FOXES' HEADS

I produced this little repeating design of foxes' heads because I find it an amusing example of the strange things the Victorians put on their patterns, things that we would never think of representing today. Who now, would produce kits showing grinning disembodied stags' heads or minute chairs, saucepans and kettles? Red-lipped, bucolic farmers are shown in all sorts of unlikely poses and landscapes and huge gloomy pieces were worked showing battlefields and the last moments of kings.

Stitched foxes' faces, or masks, turn up in all sorts of strange places and were particularly popular used on items of clothing made for Victorian husbands and suitors. I thought I would follow their example and had this waistcoat and very smart pair of slippers made for our son Nat. He intends to wear the waistcoat at school – fashion has turned full circle.

It is a simple little design to work and I have set the heads against a dark blue background as this appears to have been the colour most used with this pattern in the nineteen century. The whiskers are

By simply repeating the Foxes' Heads design on a piece of canvas marked to shape, any manner of objects can be created. The outline on the chart opposite is for men's slippers, UK sizes 6 to 10 (US sizes 7 to 11). The keyed numbers, 7–11, indicate the following:

* 7 UK size 6 (US size 7)*
* 8 UK size 7 (US size 8)*
* 9 UK size 8 (US size 9)*
10 UK size 9 (US size 10)
11 UK size 10 (US size 11)

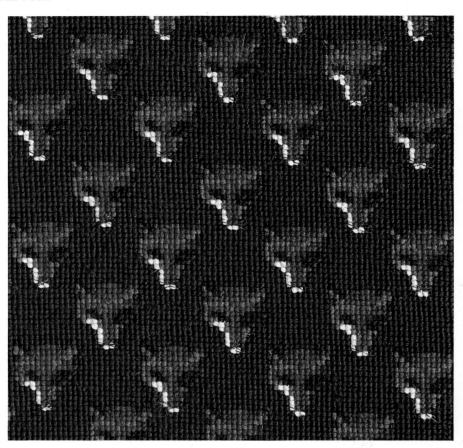

sewn in thin silk thread and are added when the piece is otherwise finished.

All sorts of small items could be made using this pattern and any number of colours used as a background. Spectacle cases, pin cushions, belts, braces or purses would all make amusing presents. A small panel of heads used as a centrepiece for one of the borders in this book could make a smart cushion for a study or library; and stool covers or chair seats would be chic if worked with black or dark hunting green backgrounds. Fox-covered smoking hats may yet become the fashion accessory of the 1990s!

FOXES' HEADS
YARN COLOURS AND QUANTITIES

The quantities are the number of yards of Elizabeth Bradley wool needed for each area of 50×20 stitches worked on 10 mesh canvas in cross stitch. (See page 164 for skein lengths of different brands.)

Key		
1	L11	12
2	G7	2
3	E11	3
4	C11	3
5	G5	3
6	F3	1

To make a pair of slippers: the quantities are the number of yards of Elizabeth Bradley wool needed if worked on 10 mesh canvas in cross stitch. (See page 164 for skein lengths of different brands.)

Key
UK size 6 (US size 7) – slightly increase quantities for larger sizes

1	L11	250
2	G7	28
3	E11	56
4	C11	51
5	G5	51
6	F3	19

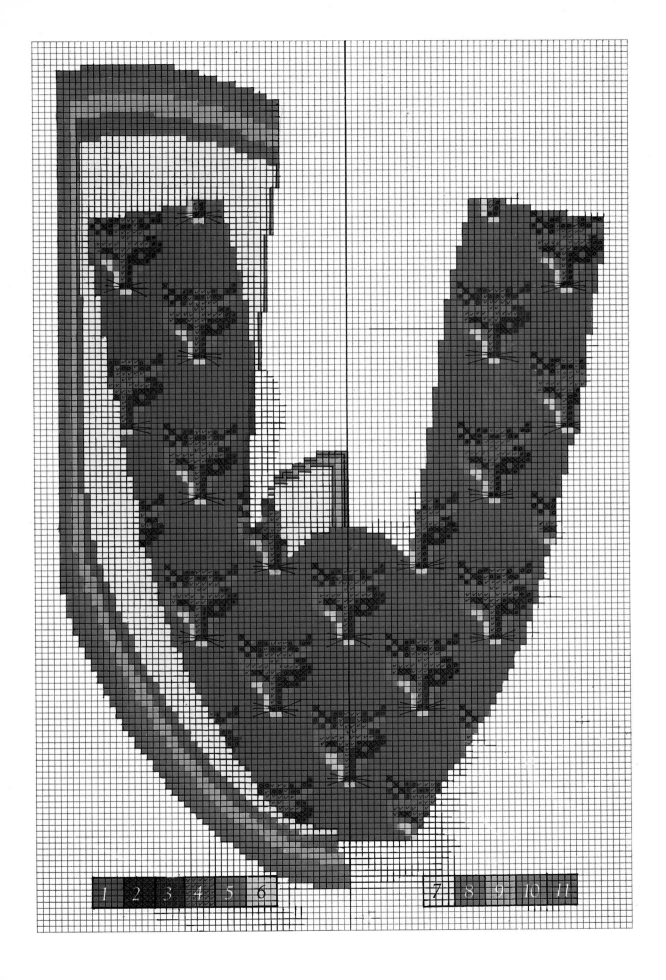

CHAPTER FIVE

....

BORDERS

*(Previous page) The Rose
and Primula Border
(photographed opposite and
charted on page 116) is a
very pretty and adaptable
border, as can be seen in this
nursery scene. It has been
used to make a small child's
cushion and a bear's
smoking hat as well as a long
bell pull doubling here as
teddy's sash.*

A border, even when it is just a simple, single line of stitches, adds an extra dimension to a piece of needlework. It defines its shape and its size. Like a length of cord or piping sewn around a cushion it gives to it a considered and finished look.

Many hundreds of border charts were produced in the nineteenth century. Some feature classic motifs such as the Greek key pattern or rows of accanthus leaves, others show interlocking geometric shapes or rococo scrolls and swirls. By far the largest group of charts shows bands of brightly coloured flowers. They are some of the earliest and prettiest of the Victorian patterns and the long painted garlands that they feature are made up of many different flowers mixed together. Roses, hollyhocks, pansies, primulas and many other varieties are intertwined in varying degrees of complexity and length.

The most obvious use of these borders is as an edging, either for a simple cushion or for a larger piece such as a wallhanging or needlework carpet. However, they can play many other decorative roles. A long flowery length of needlework makes an elegant bell pull; or when stretched across the top of a window it becomes a pelmet. Two short pieces could be shaped into a pair of curtain tie-backs. Sometimes, nineteenth-century curtains were made up in rich but plain fabrics such as velvet, serge, damask or brocade with long narrow strips of needlework attached as decoration down the inside edges and along the foot. Similar lengths could be used around the sides of squab cushions or to elaborate the edges of an upholstered stool or an otto-man lid.

Some of these flower borders were so complex that it would be a very slow process to complete a useable length. The little Rose and Primula Border (page 116) is relatively simple and quick to work, yet it is very effective and pretty. The design is based on some of the border patterns found on early nineteenth-century samplers and worked in silks on unbleached linen it could still be used as a border for a modern sampler. It would make a perfect frame for a special christening or wedding needlework.

There are two further border charts illustrated in this chapter. One features ivy leaves and curling tendrils (page 120) and the other a smart row of tassels with matching rosettes in the corners (page 121). Other border patterns are shown framing various designs in the book. For example, there are two repeating geometric borders on page 53 shown as possible edgings for a rosebud pin cushion, but either could be used to surround other items.

Another useful pattern is the narrow border which frames the Barley Twists and Cornflowers on page 99. The motif shows a line of rather classical lozenge shapes and it could be valuable for adding formality to various pieces of needlework. Suitable items might be cushion squares, the sides of bell pulls and pelmets or around any small, oblong object such as a stool or pin cushion. The design has something of the same style as the Tassel Border and could be used in combination with it to make a slightly deeper edging.

Most borders are basically long strips of needle-work made up of short sections of pattern joined together and repeated over and over again. However, the length of these repeats do vary considerably, as does the ease with which the borders can be made to turn round corners. Planning and foresight are definitely necessary before plunging in and starting to sew: the borders of many antique samplers illustrate the dangers of unplanned edgings. It is only too easy to sew away happily, reach the corner, and find there is only room left for half a pattern. I find the half honeysuckle flowers and unnaturally foreshort-ened rosebuds found at the corners of old samplers rather endearing. Half a tassel or quarter of a lozenge at a corner on a formal cushion is less charming.

Most Victorian border charts and many modern ones show the design represented as a straightforward length of pattern. Sadly they do not usually show how to get that pattern to go round a corner. Nor do they show how to make sure that the design joins up perfectly when you have worked around your centrepiece and are back at the starting point. Some of these charts can be quite awkward to use and work out. I tend to try any aid that I can think of to help me and find it helpful to photocopy a border chart several times over. The copies can then be cut into pieces and arranged in different combinations and experimental layouts. A plan drawn on graph paper is also useful. Most graph paper has 10 squares to the inch and the canvas I recommend you use also has 10 holes to the inch, and this uniformity of scale makes calculations much easier. Large sheets of graph paper can be bought from most art shops. All borders should be planned from the centre of their length outwards and if the design needs to be adapted to make the border fit exactly, this can be planned at this stage, rather than when you reach those awkward corners. (For more detailed advice see pages 150–53.)

If you wish to find some more designs with which to experiment, I suggest that you look at sampler borders and at the lines of pattern which often divide old samplers into sections. Borders on painted furniture and textiles or designs on classic freizes can all provide inspiration; Paisley shawls and wallpapers often have delightful borders. In short, it would be worth looking closely at any object that has a decorative edge design. Inspiration can come from the most unlikely sources. Borders can give your work great individuality as well as being interesting to work and pretty to look at. Finally, here is a list of some of the many items that were made using nineteenth-century border patterns. A number of these objects would still be useful today: bell pulls, decorative curtain edgings, pelmets for windows and mantelpieces, table cover and carpet borders, frames for cushion squares, edges for stools, ottoman tops, boxes or square cushions, curtain tie-backs, belts, braces, cummerbunds, spectacle cases, needle cases and dog collars.

ROSE AND PRIMULA BORDER

This classic and pretty flowered border is similar to many that were produced in the early years of Queen Victoria's reign. It shows bunches of mauve and purple primulas alternating with simple pink roses. It has a full repeat of 40 stitches and a half repeat of

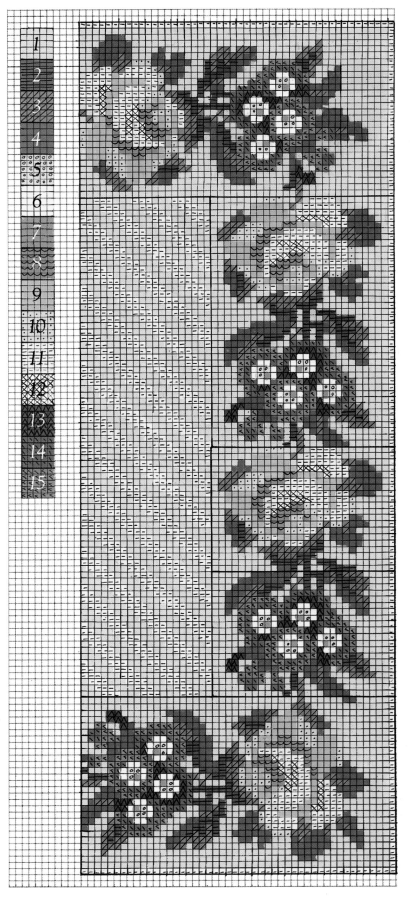

20 stitches and, like most early Victorian borders, it is quite narrow measuring 27 stitches in width.

The pattern can be used in any number of ways, the most obvious of which is as the border for a cushion or rug. As long as the central part of the piece measures a multiple of either the 40 or 20 stitches then the border is quite simple to use. As a general rule, it is always easier to increase or decrease the size of the centrepiece of the project rather than try to alter the border itself. The chart shows one side of a small cushion with a centrepiece of 80 stitches. The background area has been painted pale blue and it illustrates how this pattern can be organized to turn corners. Note the few extra leaves that have been added at each corner to fill the space and finish off the pattern. This chart was followed exactly to make the little cushion on the child's chair in the nursery scene (page 113). It is such a small piece that the centre is best kept simple and it has been worked in a basic design of diagonal pink and blue stripes, each three squares wide.

A more elaborate cushion piece is shown on page 115. The centrepiece this time measures 120 stitches and so another unit of a rose and primula has been added to each side. This time the background is worked in cream wool and a central motif design of a Basket of Roses has been added to the basic diagonal stripes. Any of the small patchwork designs from Chapter Six could be used in the same way. The Posy of Violets (page 64) or the Rosebud Wreath (page 53) would both make most attractive alternatives to put in the middle of such a cushion.

As a long band of flowers, the pattern could be used to make bell pulls, braces or belts. In the nursery scene on page 113 the largest bear wears a pale blue bell pull as a girdle and a smoking hat to match. The top of the hat is sewn with the same diagonal stripes as the centre of the cushion and a traditional dangling silk tassel has been added to complete the effect. Advice is given on page 150 as to how to successfully plan this border.

ROSE AND PRIMULA BORDER
YARN COLOURS AND QUANTITIES

The quantities are the number of yards of Elizabeth Bradley wool needed for each repeat of 27×40 stitches worked on 10 mesh canvas in cross stitch.

(See page 164 for skein lengths of different brands.)
Multiply the quantities by the number of times the
complete pattern is repeated on the piece you plan
to make.

Key		
1	L1	7
2	J8	1
3	I8	2
4	J6	3
5	D4	½
6	C2	1
7	C6	½
8	A5	1
9	A4	2
10	B4	1
11	B3	2
12	B2	1
13	N8	½
14	N10	1
15	N6	1

IVY LEAVES

Long trailing strands of ivy with dark green leaves
and curling tendrils can be seen on many Victorian
charts. The simple and distinctive form of the leaves

*Trailing ivy leaves make a
decorative border.*

The Ivy Leaves border is smart and useful, especially for making long strips of leafy woolwork for bell pulls or edgings. The chair seat and cushion centre are worked in the same geometric design, based on folded ribbons.

Ivy patterns are decorative, but restrained in colour and form and can add interest and style to pieces made from some of the repeating geometric patterns of which I am particularly fond. Such a combination can be seen opposite. The simple central pattern of folded ribbons echoes the colours of the ivy leaves and the border adds interest to what would be a rather plain cushion if the central design was used alone. The centrepiece and its surround complement each other perfectly, whereas a more elaborate flowered border could jar and a simple geometric edging be merely dull.

This particular ivy border is based on an original chart that had been stuck into a small Victorian scrapbook of designs and patterns. This delightful and much used volume was lent to me by Miss Bette Anderson. Like many of the early Victorian borders it is quite narrow being only 28 stitches wide and it has a long repeat of 92 stitches. It would therefore make an ideal bell pull. These long strips of needlework can be very decorative in a modern room. They are also extremely useful for brightening up awkward narrow pieces of wall. Hung on either side of a fireplace or next to a door or window they can look most attractive.

Bell pulls were part of the normal fixtures and fittings of a Victorian house. They hung in most rooms used by the family and could be pulled when the assistance of a servant was required. Each bell pull was connected to a network of wires running from rooms all over the house to a row of polished metal bells hanging in the kitchen. These often varied in size so that each made a different sound. A musical housemaid would know which bell was ringing from its tone without having to look to see which one was moving. Bell pulls were a very practical application for Berlin woolwork. The completed strips of needlework were strong, hardwearing and attractive. Special brass fittings were available for sewing onto the ends – typically, an ornate ring at the top and a matching handle at the bottom although sometimes an elaborate handmade tassel was used instead of a handle.

Because it has a long repeat, this border is less adaptable as a cushion or rug edging than the other borders shown in the book. It will turn corners, but not easily or exactly and it was with some difficulty

makes a useful contrast to the colourful luxuriance of many of the Victorian flower designs.

that I managed to organize the border of the cushion shown (see page 153 for more detailed advice). I had intended to make this piece an exact square but eventually I had to compromise and settle for an oblong shape.

I worked the mixture of blue green and olive leaves against a brick red background. The Victorians often used a particularly attractive slightly brighter red which is a mixture between vermillion and coral. Sapphire blue, pale blue or the ever-popular black and cream would all make successful backgrounds.

The centre of this chart is based on a popular and decorative geometric design from the same early Victorian period as the border. It is worked in the same colours with the addition of orange. I am particularly fond of these geometric patterns as centre pieces but a pictorial subject could be used instead. A small landscape or a flower arrangement would be pretty.

IVY LEAVES
YARN COLOURS AND QUANTITIES
BORDER

The quantities are the number of yards of Elizabeth Bradley wool needed for each repeat of 92×28 stitches worked on 10 mesh canvas in cross stitch. (See page 164 for skein lengths of different brands.) Multiply the quantities by the number of times the complete pattern is repeated on the piece you plan to make.

Key		
1 (rust)	B7	24
or		
2 (red)	B10	24
3	I10	6
4	I8	7
5	I5	6
6	J4	5
7	K5	4
8	K4	5

CENTREPIECE

The quantities are the number of yards of Elizabeth Bradley wool needed for each area of 30×30 stitches worked on 10 mesh canvas in cross stitch. (See page 164 for skein lengths of different brands.)

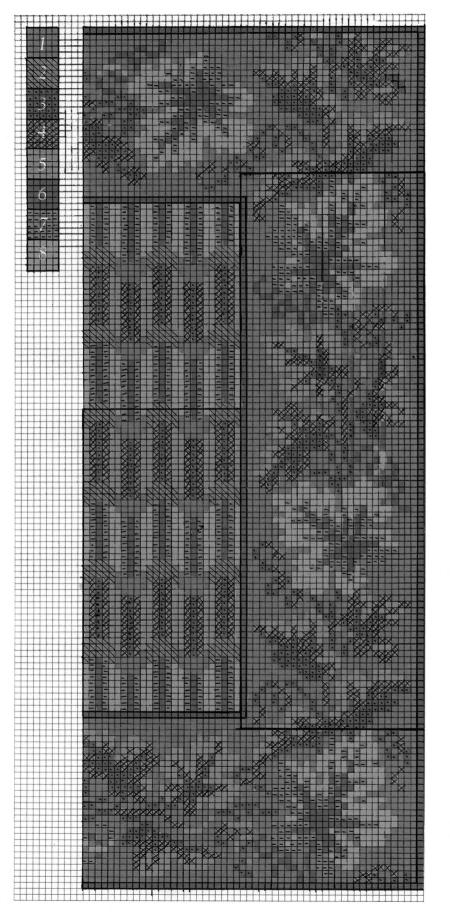

Key
1 (rust)	B7	2
or		
2 (red)	B10	2
2	C6	2
3	I10	2
4	I8	4
5	I5	4
6	J4	2
7	K5	4
8	K4	4

TASSEL BORDER

This border is a great favourite of mine. I first saw it used on a particularly fine piece of Victorian wool-work where it formed a band down both sides. It is a rather classical design and adds a touch of formality to any piece of needlework that it surrounds.

As can be seen in the photograph on page 123 it looks very smart used as a cover for the sides of a square Georgian stool or it could be made into edges for a box cushion or ottoman top. A tasselled pelmet with matching curtain tie-backs would suit a small study or library and a tasselled smoking hat could start a whole new fashion. The tassels themselves can be made longer or shorter depending on the width of the strip of needlework that is needed. Tassels of more than about 4 inches (10cm) might look a little odd, however.

This design has a repeat of only 10 stitches which means that it can be used to surround practically any cushion square or rug centrepiece. A few single rows of stitches or narrow stripes worked in different coloured wools can be added around the edge of the central area to increase its size if necessary. This border design, like many others, proved somewhat awkward to manoeuvre round a right angle easily. However, the addition of a rosette as a separate corner motif worked well as an alternative – I think it adds to the decorative quality of the border as a whole. I used an oak leaf green as a background for both models. Many colours could be used, but the more traditional greens, blues, creams, black or reds look the most effective. The tassels can be worked in the colours shown on the chart, which are very close to the shades used in the original piece of wool-work. Other mixtures can be used if preferred.

Some of the geometric designs featured earlier in

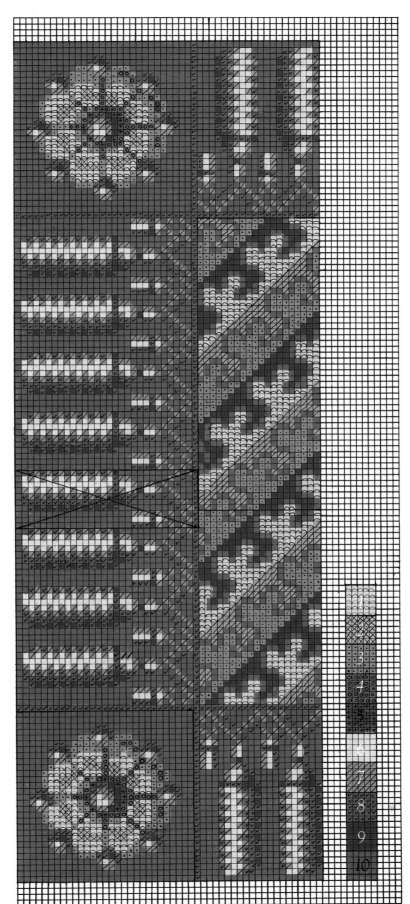

the book would make restrained and decorative stool tops or cushion centres while this border would make a fine edging. Advice is given on page 152 on this border.

TASSEL BORDER
YARN COLOURS AND QUANTITIES

The quantities are the number of yards of Elizabeth Bradley wool needed for each repeat of 29×10 stitches worked on 10 mesh canvas in cross stitch. (See page 164 for skein lengths of different brands.) To establish how much yarn is needed, multiply the quantities below by the number of times the complete pattern is repeated on the piece you plan to make.

Key

6	C2	2
7	C6	2
8	C11	2
9	E12	½
10	J8	3

ROSETTES
YARN COLOURS AND QUANTITIES

The quantities are the number of yards of Elizabeth Bradley wool needed for each rosette worked on 10 mesh canvas in cross stitch. (See page 164 for skein lengths of different brands.)

Key

1	E1	2
2	C1	1
3	E2	2
4	G5	½
5	G6	½
6	C2	½
7	C6	1
8	C11	1
9	E12	½
10	J8	8 .

CENTREPIECE

The quantities are the number of yards of Elizabeth Bradley wool needed for each area of 50×20 stitches (or any other 10sq in [25sq cm] combination) worked on 10 mesh canvas in cross stitch. (See page 164 for skein lengths of different brands.)

Key

1	E1	5
3	E2	5
7	C6	5
9	E12	5
10	J8	5

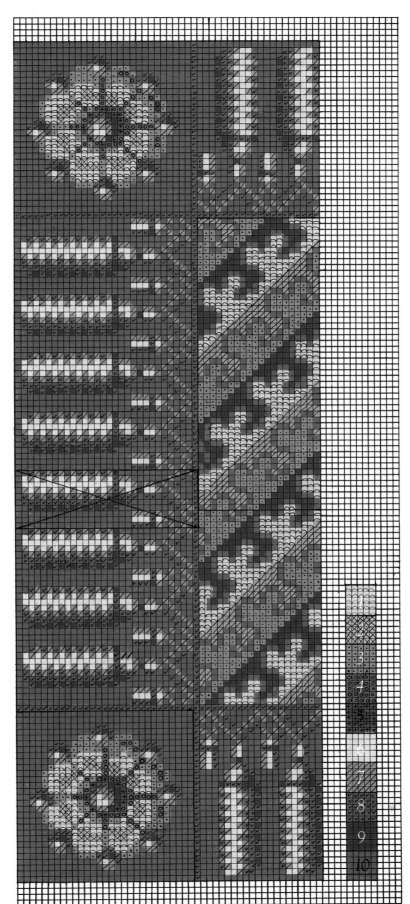

121

*(Previous page and right)
The Tassel Border is one of
my favourite border designs.
It adds great style to
whatever it surrounds. Here
it has been used to edge a
cushion with a geometric
centrepiece worked in
complementary colours. A
classical rosette has been
stitched at each corner. The
same border, but with
slightly elongated tassels,
has been used to make the
sides of the footstool.*

CHAPTER SIX

....

PATCHWORK PIECES AND NEEDLEWORK CARPETS

(Previous page) This picture shows a whole array of needlework made from my designs. Some pieces have been joined together to make carpets, while others have been made into cushions, stool covers and bell pulls. Many different background colours are shown and it is interesting to see how much they affect the look of the finished pieces.

The Lion (see chart on page 140).

There is a rather interesting group of Berlin charts that were produced in the early years of the nineteenth century. They show a whole variety of tiny designs reminiscent of the motifs still stitched on to the corners of embroidered Swiss handkerchiefs. Each chart is completely covered with small patterns or pictures, either arranged in neat rows, or scattered randomly over the sheet of paper. The painting and quality of the designs is generally excellent and the patterns can look charming framed as pictures.

There seems to have been a wide choice of subject material, some charts were produced singly while others form part of a series. One such series includes patterns featuring rows of tiny figures all dressed in different regional costumes. Others show animals and children playing in miniature landscapes complete with mountains, chalets and castles. Another unusual and rather distinctive type of chart is covered by scattered representations of many minute objects. Kettles, flower wreaths, garden forks and spades, guns and hunting horns are all mixed together in a haphazard arrangement on the page.

As far as I can see after many years spent viewing sales and searching for needlework to buy, these small designs appear to have had two main applications. One of these was for use as spot motifs on children's samplers and the other was as the centrepieces of small pieces of Berlin woolwork that were then joined together to make larger areas of patchwork

Cornucopia (see chart on page 134).

or mosaic needlework.

Most early charts were produced in Berlin and they were made first and foremost for the use of German needlewomen. Germany has its own distinctive style of needlework, as does every country. Samplers, in particular, can be recognized immediately as coming from one country or another. They vary in the way they are planned and laid out and in their shape, colours and motifs. Different textures and colours of linen are used and even the silk or wool threads have national characteristics.

German and Dutch samplers share many similarities and are very different from British examples. They are less strictly organized, and the main body of the piece is normally covered by a whole mass of little designs which fill the rectangle outlined by a simple border. Many of the small motifs appear over and over again on different samplers of this type. The children who made them must have enjoyed working the little chairs, kettles and other homely motifs as well as the more usual wreaths of flowers, landscapes and animals.

Some of these motifs were taken from earlier samplers and pattern books, but many nineteenth-century sampler makers no doubt used the new Berlin charts as well. Since exactly the same small designs appear so often, it seems likely that some of the charts that they came from were given away as 'free inserts' in the ladies' magazines of the day. From about 1840 onwards some identical motifs appear on

British and American samplers, particularly the romantic little vignettes of landscapes and views. A pair of designs showing a little girl skipping and a companion boy with a hoop, both set against naturalistic scenes, appear to have been particularly appealing as they were used so frequently.

The more pictoral and elaborate examples of this type of chart were also used as the centres for small, regular-shaped pieces of woolwork. These pieces could be joined together to make larger pieces of needlework rather in the way that fabric shapes are joined together to make a patchwork quilt. As in such quilts, the shapes can be joined in a number of ways so as to create different patterns.

This sort of woolwork is generally of fine quality and judging from the background colours and general style it was obviously made during the early years of the Berlin work craze. Often the central motif is stitched in petit point while the background is worked in a larger cross stitch. These patchwork pieces are most commonly square in shape and they are usually joined by a single line of stitches in a contrasting colour. The various pieces were stitched separately and then sewn together when they were all completed – the join was achieved by overlapping the edges of the canvas and working the connecting rows through both pieces. Several lines of stitches make a stronger joint and three rows was usual. These three rows of stitches could be made up of two rows of the background colour and one of another colour acting as a dividing line, or all three could be different acting as a decorative stripe between the squares. An area of completed woolwork of this type rather resembles an expanse of Delft tiles each with a different picture painted in the centre. Just as Delft tiles sometimes have a small painted decoration at each corner so the squares are often elaborated by the addition of a little rococo scroll at each corner. It is easy to see why patchwork woolwork is often called tile or mosaic needlework.

Occasionally, the central motif is worked diagonally across the square and the pieces are then joined together as if they were a set of interlocking diamonds. Hexagons were another popular basic geometric shape. They were either joined simply, as in a grandmother's flower garden patchwork quilt, or with a diamond added in between each hexagon as an intervening shape. Either arrangement is most attractive. As the design is more complex than

joined squares or diamonds such pieces were often worked on one large piece of canvas. This avoided any possible difficulties in joining separate pieces together later.

Among the many squares of woolwork that I have purchased over the years, several stand out in my mind. One was a very fine quality piece that had never been finished and was sold still attached to its mahogany working frame. The whole thing was worked in a mixture of wool and silk on a fine meshed piece of canvas, probably about 14 or 15 holes to the inch. The basic hexagon shapes were outlined with a single line of Royal blue cross stitch worked in wool with intervening diamond shapes worked in rust, black and yellow; the yellow being silk and the other two colours wool. The area inside the hexagons had not yet been stitched but pinned in the centre of each space was a tiny Berlin pattern cut out from a large sheet. Some unknown event had obviously prevented the completion of what would have been a most decorative piece.

Another charming example of patchwork embroidery consisted of twelve small squares joined together and in the centre of each was stitched a tiny animal in minute petit point. The background was worked in a pale tan colour and the design was elaborated by the addition of a triangle which fitted into the corner of each square. These little triangles were each made up of three stripes worked in pale

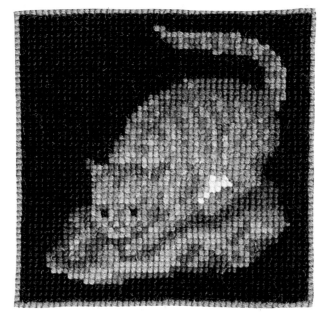

The Cat (see chart on page 135).

The Swan (see chart on page 139).

pink, mid pink and faded crimson wool. A black line had been used to edge each square. On the joined and finished piece the corner triangles formed a diamond shape where each of the four squares met.

I am particularly fond of all types of patchwork or tile needlework. It is attractive and interesting and so original pieces are widely sought after and invariably expensive when discovered. Quite large panels were sometimes constructed and there is a sofa in the Welsh Folk Museum at St Fagans, Cardiff that is completely covered by delightful small designs worked on squares joined together.

This type of needlework can also be used to cover large folding screens. The various pieces can be made by many different people and then joined together. This means that quite ambitious community or group projects can be considered. The Heritage Tapestry organized by Kaffe Fassett is one such undertaking. Over 2,500 6-inch (15-cm) squares of needlework were sent in by television viewers from all over Britain. They worked to a basic theme of 'count your blessings' and the charming and lively little squares that they made were edged and then made into a fourteen-panel screen which is regularly on public display. Similar screens were made in the nineteenth century and very occasionally they come on the market. I remember one particularly magnificent example, which when fully extended must have been at least 20 feet long. The

panels were 6 feet (2m) high and they were completely covered by hundreds of 5-inch (12.5-cm) squares each featuring a different Berlin woolwork design. Flowers, animals and landscapes were the most frequent subjects, each different, and all worked against a black background. Three lines of rust and yellow divide the squares.

For this book I painted nine little charts which I thought would be fun for you to sew. Each completed piece can be used to make small objects such as pin cushions, dolls' house carpets and small pictures, or they could be joined together to make a patchwork cushion. If more 'patches' are required, geometric patterns can make interesting alternative squares. Pieces featuring initials and dates can add individuality and small square sections of some of the repeating patterns are another possibility.

When the squares are completed and before you start to join them together, do check that they all contain the same number of rows of stitches. If they do not, they will never join together properly so it is worth undoing or adding any necessary rows at this stage rather than have problems later.

Needlework carpets can be made on much the same principle as a piece of patchwork needlework. The separate pieces, though bigger in size, are joined in the much same way. A carpet needs to be planned carefully and the pieces tacked together before working the connecting rows. Again, great care must be taken to ensure that each of the carpet squares measures exactly the correct number of stitches. Further instructions on carpet making are given on pages 154–5.

Needlework carpets were, of course, made long before the nineteenth century though it was not until then that they were worked in any great numbers. Some exquisite carpets have survived from the seventeenth and eighteenth centuries. As a rule they were worked by expert needlewomen and were made all in one piece on large frames. They were normally sewn in tent stitch on canvas, using crewel wools although silk was sometimes used to highlight portions of the design. Many of these pieces are still in superb condition as they were often used as table carpets rather than floor coverings. They were probably kept in the dark for much of their lives and brought out for special occasions. Even so, considering their age, it is surprising how many have survived to this day.

In contrast, nineteenth-century woolwork carpets were usually made by amateurs. Some were made in one piece but many more were constructed from individual squares stitched together. This very practical method of construction and the easy availability of suitable patterns and materials led to a huge increase in production. The finished pieces were not only decorative but strong and hardwearing and many are still in use well over a hundred years after they were made.

Some carpets were group projects with many people making the various squares. Several such projects were documented – for example a carpet of 63 squares each containing a design of flowers or a bird was made by Miss Wallis and her friends and then given to her god daughter Emily Ann Powell on the occasion of her marriage in 1851. A famous carpet was designed by the architect JW Papworth which was presented to Queen Victoria. It consisted of 150 2-foot (60-cm) squares which had been joined to form a carpet of 20×30 feet (6×9m). The squares were worked with a mixture of flower designs and geometric patterns and the border included the heraldic devices of all the needlewomen involved in the project. It was exhibited at the Great Exhibition in 1851 since when it has sadly disappeared without trace. A third example was worked by the ladies of the diocese of Gloucester and presented to the Bishop in 1843. It was 22 feet (6.5m) long and consisted of 77 panels. Baskets and bunches of flowers

were stitched on alternate brown and cream squares, and the episcopal coat of arms was neatly worked in the centre.

I first saw nineteenth-century needlework carpets in any numbers in the London salerooms during the late 1970s and early 1980s. Berlin woolwork had just become fashionable and it was popular with antique dealers and collectors. Pieces were readily available in large numbers and prices were very reasonable. Although I was mainly buying samplers at that time I remember clearly the period when a whole selection of absolutely gorgeous Berlin woolwork carpets seem to appear quite suddenly in the auction rooms. I suspect that they had been included in carpet sales rather than needlework auctions before that time. Some of them were quite stunning and they seemed to sell for vast prices. We needlework dealers watched in total fascination as interior decorators and carpet dealers battled for ownership of some of the more magnificent pieces.

I was amazed by the size of some of these rugs. It is one thing to read that huge salon carpets were made and another to actually see one – especially when one remembers that each stitch was worked by an industrious Victorian lady. Attractive, original nineteenth-century carpets can still be found in various states of repair in salerooms and antique shops. There are specialist dealers both in London and New York selling original pieces and several of

(Top) Bunch of Flowers (see chart on page 134).

(Bottom) The Horse (see chart on page 138).

(Top) Rose Wreath (see chart on page 133).

(Bottom) The Spaniel (see chart on page 138).

(Opposite) A patchwork carpet featuring various Elizabeth Bradley designs of which the Parrot is charted on page 24.

them offer excellent modern copies and adaptations of Victorian rugs. Other ready-made examples can be obtained from decorators who specialize in interiors using antiques and we produce finished carpets made locally in Wales by a workforce of over one hundred needlemen and women.

Although I am delighted that such carpets are available and that a long tradition is being continued, I am even more pleased that so many stitchers want to make their own carpets. They manage to find the time somehow in their busy lives to tackle such ambitious projects and seem to derive enormous pleasure from them. I always intended that whatever kits I produced, they could each be incorporated into rugs as well as being useful for the more normal cushions, pictures and chair seats. I am delighted that so many of our customers are making pieces of various shapes and sizes and apparently enjoying it. We get to hear details of some of their projects. One needleman in Maryland is making a 36-panel carpet with an elephant in each corner – two are facing one way and two are reversed so that all four face inwards. A group of six ladies, also in America, all got together to make a 12-panel animal rug as a surprise present for a close friend who could not sew. What a birthday present! Many others are making mixed subject carpets, runners for their halls, pretty flower carpets or hearth rugs made from two squares with a border. A carpet does not

have to be large – a little flower rug next to a bed or in front of a fire can be charming and seems a much more attainable project. You can always make your stair carpet or drawing room centrepiece later.

PATCHWORK PIECES

Beside each chapter heading in this book there is a miniscule charted design and in the photograph on page 141 all nine of these little designs are shown worked on black backgrounds and then joined together to make an elaborate tasselled cushion.

I have called these designs Patchwork Pieces because they are joined together in a similar fashion to the little scraps of patterned fabric sewn together to make a patchwork quilt. Each square of the woolwork patchwork cushion featured here is joined to the next by two rows of ochre wool with a line of olive green stitches between them. The method of joining canvas pieces is given on page 153.

Many of the Victorian chart makers produced sheets of charts covered with such small designs. They were often worked in petit point on small square or hexagonal pieces of canvas and then joined together to make large panels of needlework, which were used to cover stools and ottomans or large folding screens. The tiny patterns were also used to embellish many of the small items of fancy work that were given away as gifts or sold at charity bazaars.

The Rose Basket which is charted opposite.

The designs have been photographed against a whole mass of sewing paraphernalia: buttons, wools, tassels, needles, and all sorts of interesting bits and pieces. Among all this are pin cushions made from the designs worked against different colour backgrounds. The Swan is set against pale green wool and The Lion and Rose Basket against cream. There is also a selection of the little Rose Wreath design sewn on canvases of different mesh sizes and with various sorts of yarns. These small examples were made to show how much difference these factors make to the look and size of the finished pieces. There are two Rose Wreaths worked in cross stitch on 10 mesh interlock canvas. One is framed and the other is part of the main cushion. There is an example worked in half cross stitch on double threaded 10 mesh Penelope canvas which looks similar except the pattern is slightly less bold and distinct because of the stitch used. Another most attractive version has been sewn onto 14 mesh mono canvas using cross stitch worked in crewel wool. The last little square shows a tiny wreath sewn in pale silks onto 20 mesh natural unbleached linen scrim. It would make a pretty greetings card or sampler motif.

These small designs can also be used as the central motifs for small cushions, perhaps surrounded by one of the borders featured earlier in the book. The Rose and Primula border (page 116) with the little Rose Basket motif shown opposite is particularly successful.

ROSE WREATH
YARN COLOURS AND QUANTITIES

The quantities are the number of yards of Elizabeth Bradley wool needed for each square of 50×50 stitches worked on 10 mesh canvas in cross stitch. (See page 164 for skein lengths of different brands.)

Key		
1	J8	4
2	J4	5
3	J6	4
4	A4	3
5	A3	3
6	B4	3
7	B2	1
Background: 1 hank		

ROSE BASKET
YARN COLOURS AND QUANTITIES

The quantities are the number of yards of Elizabeth Bradley wool needed for each square of 50×50 stitches worked on 10 mesh canvas in cross stitch. (See page 164 for skein lengths of different brands.)

Key		
1	A4	2
2	A3	4
3	A2	5
4	B1	2
5	J8	4
6	J6	5
7	I4	7
8	G5	2
9	E4	3
10	E2	3
Background: 1 hank		

BUNCH OF FLOWERS
YARN COLOURS AND QUANTITIES

The quantities are the number of yards of Elizabeth Bradley wool needed for each square of 50×50 stitches worked on 10 mesh canvas in cross stitch. (See page 164 for skein lengths of different brands.)

Key		
1	N1	2
2	N11	1

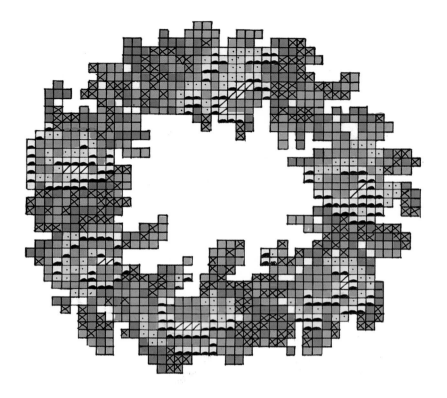

Rose Wreath.

Rose Basket.

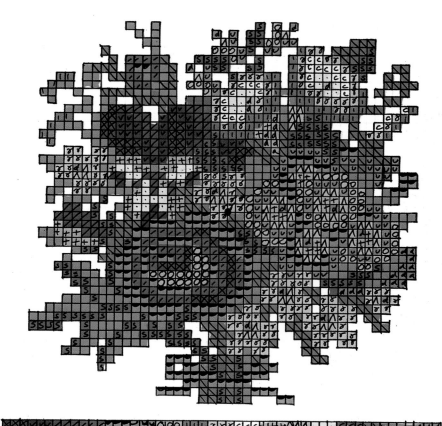

Bunch of Flowers.

Cornucopia.

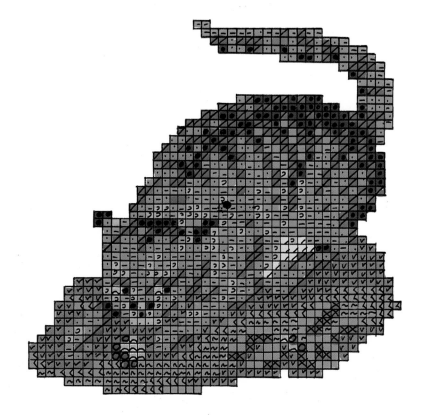

The Cat.

1	2	3	4	5	6	7	8	9	10	11	12	13	14

3	N10	1
4	A4	2
5	A3	4
6	A2	2
7	B2	3
8	L3	3
9	L2	4
10	K1	1
11	C3	1
12	C2	3
13	C1	2
14	J8	4
15	K5	4
16	J4	4
17	I6	2

Background: 1 hank

Key		
1	J8	4
2	J4	7
3	L3	4
4	L2	4
5	K1	2
6	C3	1
7	C2	1
8	C1	2
9	F8	3
10	E4	3
11	E2	4

Background: 1 hank

CORNUCOPIA
YARN COLOURS AND QUANTITIES

The quantities are the number of yards of Elizabeth Bradley wool needed for each square of 50×50 stitches worked on 10 mesh canvas in cross stitch. (See page 164 for skein lengths of different brands.)

THE CAT
YARN COLOURS AND QUANTITIES

The quantities are the number of yards of Elizabeth Bradley wool needed for each square of 50×50 stitches worked on 10 mesh canvas in cross stitch. (See page 164 for skein lengths of different brands.)

Key		
1	H5	3
2	F9	5

138

*(Previous page) Nine small
designs have here been
joined together to make a
cushion. They can also be
used separately to make a
whole range of little pieces,
small examples of which can
be seen scattered among the
haberdashery in the picture.*

The Horse.

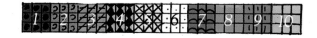

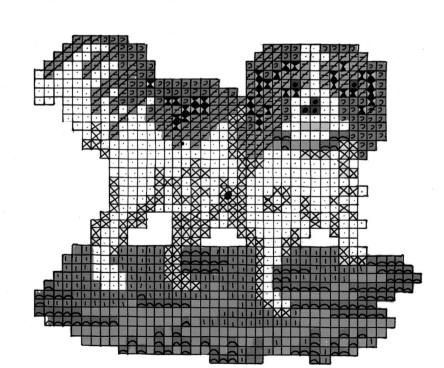

The Spaniel.

The Swan.

3	H3	5	
4	E5	4	
5	E2	2	
6	F3	1	
7	A9	1	
8	N1	1	
9	N3	1	
10	I11	4	
11	I8	2	
12	I3	2	
13	J8	1	
14	I6	1	
eyes	G11	1	

Background: 1 hank

THE HORSE
YARN COLOURS AND QUANTITIES

The quantities are the number of yards of Elizabeth Bradley wool needed for each square of 50×50 stitches worked on 10 mesh canvas in cross stitch.

(See page 164 for skein lengths of different brands.)

Key

1	G7	3
2	E12	6
3	E9	6
4	E7	4
5	E5	1
6	I8	3
7	I3	6

Background: 1 hank

THE SPANIEL
YARN COLOURS AND QUANTITIES

The quantities are the number of yards of Elizabeth Bradley wool needed for each square of 50×50 stitches worked on 10 mesh canvas in cross stitch. (See page 164 for skein lengths of different brands.)

Key

1	G7	1
2	E9	2

A completed patchwork cushion made from the nine small patterns offers variety and yet the pieces complement each other in terms of colour and design.

The Lion.

3	E7	4
4	E5	1
5	C1	3
6	F3	6
7	J8	3
8	I6	3
9	I8	3
10	A9	1

Background: 1 hank

THE SWAN
YARN COLOURS AND QUANTITIES

The quantities are the number of yards of Elizabeth Bradley wool needed for each square of 50×50 stitches worked on 10 mesh canvas in cross stitch. (See page 164 for skein lengths of different brands.)

Key

1	G11	1
2	H7	5
3	H6	8
4	F2	9
5	B4	1
6	L2	3

| 7 | L1 | 3 |
| Background: 1 hank | | |

THE LION
YARN COLOURS AND QUANTITIES

The quantities are the number of yards of Elizabeth Bradley wool needed for each square of 50×50 stitches worked on 10 mesh canvas in cross stitch. (See page 164 for skein lengths of different brands.)

Key

1	G6	1
2	E7	1
3	E10	4
4	E5	6
5	E4	4
6	E2	2
7	F6	7
8	B4	1
9	N1	1
10	I7	2
11	J8	2
12	J6	3

Background: 1 hank

MATERIALS AND METHODS

CANVAS

Embroidery can be defined as any form of decorative stitchery worked with thread onto some sort of fabric. Many materials can be used but, traditionally, certain types predominated. In the nineteenth century, silk or fine gauze was used as a base for more delicate projects, which were usually pictures or exquisitely embellished garments. Children sewed their samplers on linen or woollen cloth called tammy. Bed linen, curtains and hangings were – and are – made of embroidered linen and it is only recently that decorated table and tray-cloths ceased to be part of every well appointed bride's bottom drawer. Until the mid-nineteenth century, woolwork was normally done on an open weave fabric similar to modern sackcloth. Some needlework carpets today are still made on this hessian. It can be left unworked as a background for needlework pictures.

Although the charts from this book can be used to embroider pictures on any of the materials above, they are primarily intended to be worked with wool onto special machine-woven canvas. The first such canvas was a double-threaded variety called Penelope canvas. It was easy to use and could be made in different sizes and widths. It is still popular today and has remained virtually identical in type to when it was first produced.

The Victorians had a vast range of different canvases to choose from but over the years they have become standardized and many of the more exotic colours and weaves have been discontinued. Today's canvases can be divided into three main types: double threaded (Penelope canvas), single

thread (mono canvas), and the relatively recent interlock canvas. All are made in a variety of mesh sizes and widths and except for interlock are generally supplied in a choice of colours. The most readily available is white, then there is natural brown, unbleached, canvas which is sometimes known as antique, and an off-white version called cream or ecru. Interlock canvas is only made in white which is a pity as a natural canvas is more aesthetically pleasing and white threads show through the stitching far more than on darker ones. This means that far more care has to be taken to cover the canvas well with the stitches.

All these canvases are described or measured by the number of mesh per inch (a mesh being the intersection where each two threads cross). Ten mesh canvas has ten threads and ten holes per inch.

The first of the three types of canvas, Penelope canvas, is smooth and double threaded. It is flat, firm and easy to work upon as the threads of the canvas remain in place and do not slide about as the stitches are made. It can be used for both cross stitch and half cross stitch. An additional advantage of Penelope is that petit and gros point can both be worked on the same piece of canvas. Details such as faces or the centres of flowers can be worked over one thread in tiny stitches while the main area can be covered with larger stitches worked over both threads together. Most Victorian Berlin woolwork was done on 10 mesh Penelope canvas. It was normally worked in cross stitch, sometimes mixed with areas of petit point.

The second sort of canvas, mono, is a conventional single threaded canvas which is available in a large range of colours and sizes. The best quality is made of natural and unbleached cotton threads. It is made in France and has a smooth polished appearance. Mono is a particularly strong and sturdy canvas, and most of the individually hand-painted designs are painted on it. It has many devotees and some needleworkers would not use any other sort. Personally, I find it difficult to use as the threads tend to slide about as one works. The stitches have to be made very deliberately with the hand alternately in front and behind the canvas pushing the needle to and fro and it is best used on a frame. As I like to work exclusively from the front of the canvas and very quickly, it does not suit me at all. It is possible to work cross stitch on to it, but it is a much slower process than working on a piece of Penelope or interlock canvas.

The third and newest type of canvas is called interlock and is a white cotton mono canvas with one major difference from the others – instead of the threads passing under and over one another, they actually pass through each other where they intersect, creating a firm, immovable grid. The surface is very smooth like a Penelope canvas and it is extremely easy to work upon. The holes of a 10 mesh canvas are large enough to take cross stitch worked in a modern 4-ply tapestry wool and the 12 mesh size is perfect for half cross stitch or tent stitch. It is a good canvas for beginners to use as good, even work can be achieved after very little practice.

When I was creating my first design, I tried out every type of canvas that I could get hold of. Penelope was the most obvious choice because it was the most authentic type of canvas and would have been used by the Victorians. However, modern tapestry wool is thicker than nineteenth-century Berlin wool and the holes of 10 mesh Penelope canvas are too small for cross stitch to be worked easily through them. As I wanted the finished pieces of needlework to look as much like the originals as possible, I needed a smooth 10 mesh canvas with a slightly bigger hole. Interlock fitted the bill perfectly and I am sure that Victorians would have been firm advocates if it had been invented earlier.

Whatever canvas you choose, always buy sufficient to allow at least a 3in (7.5cm) margin around the finished piece. Before starting to stitch, many people bind the edges of their canvas with masking tape. This is essential with mono canvas because it frays easily and it is advisable with both Penelope and interlock canvas as the outer edges can be quite jagged and the yarn can snag on them.

The shape and size of a piece of woolwork can become distorted in a number of ways. One of these is that if the selvedge is at the top or bottom the piece will tend to become slighty elongated. When stitching, the selvedge should always run up the side of the work so that the finished piece will end up a better and squarer shape. This is especially important if it is destined to be part of a carpet (see information on page 154).

YARNS

The traditional yarns for embroidery are normally made from wool, silk or cotton. They come in many varieties and weights, and in a whole multitude of colours. A particularly large selection was available to Victorian ladies from the needlework shops called Berlin repositories and the advertisements that these shops placed in women's journals of the day conjure up a wonderful picture of rich treasure houses filled with all manner of different threads.

In comparison, the range of yarns available today may seem rather limited but the situation is improving all the time. Renewed interest in the many different techniques of embroidery has resulted in the re-emergence of many apparently obsolete materials. Once again, it is possible to buy not only pure silk threads of various types but also multicolour beads and chenille yarns. Added to these are all the exotic textured knitting wools that can also be used for embroidery, they can be great fun to use in experimental pieces of needlework. Beads and silk can be used to highlight parts of more conventional types of woolwork but normally most of this type of needlepoint is worked in one of the main three categories of wool – tapestry wool, crewel wool or Persian yarn. All three are made by several manufacturers and they are all widely available in a good range of colours.

Tapestry wool is a soft 4-ply wool which is pleasant to use. It resembles the Berlin wool used in the nineteenth century but it is slightly thicker and stronger. Crewel wool is a thinner 2-ply wool and several strands together are necessary to cover a 10 mesh canvas. The last type, Persian yarn, is made up of three strands of wool that can be easily separated. It is very popular with many stitchers as the thickness can be varied by removing or adding a strand. It is usually slightly harder and more lustrous than tapestry wool.

We have our own range of selected tapestry wool in over 150 colours. Some of these wools are brightly coloured but most are slightly muted shades so that the resulting work has a rich antique look – not too faded, but not brilliant or garish either. Since most traditional furnishing fabrics use a similar range of colours, needlework made using our wools will fit into most room schemes. However, the charts in this book, especially the geometric patterns and repeating designs can be used with your own choice of colours rather than mine as you may prefer pale pastel colours or bright primary shades. Experimenting with a variety of different ranges of colours to see how differing effects can be created is always worthwhile.

Apart from the three main types of wool, various sorts of silk and cotton threads are available. One of the most popular is a stranded perle cotton which resembles silk. A duller and thicker cotton used for Scandinavian embroidery can also be useful for many sorts of needlework. I love using pure silk thread, it has such a smooth, luxurious feel and the colours are often exceptionally good.

YARN QUANTITIES

The wool quantities given in this book are for the number of yards needed of Elizabeth Bradley 4-ply tapestry wool, if working in the cross stitch shown on page 146, on a 10 mesh, interlock canvas. These quantities could be approximately halved if half cross stitch or tent stitch is used. Remember that the finer the mesh, the greater the amount of yarn that will be used.

Most of the designs in this book are new and in most cases only one prototype of each chart has been worked. Consequently the wool quantities given with each design are strictly approximate. Normally I would have five or six examples of each worked and then average all the lengths of wool that the different needleworkers used to get a more accurate picture of quantities required. It is surprising how much these can vary and the more complicated the design, the greater are the differences. Once the average has been estimated I normally add 30 per

cent to allow for mistakes and unusual methods of working. The quantities printed in this book take into account this addition.

Weight is used as the standard unit for wool. Yarns are bought in ounces or grammes rather than yards or metres. Because the different brands and thicknesses of wool weigh different amounts, the various skeins, hanks and balls all contain different lengths of thread. The conversion chart on page 164 has been devised to help with the calculations of how much wool to purchase if you wish to use wool other than that supplied by Elizabeth Bradley. Most needleworkers have bags of wool left over from other projects and some of this can be utilized. Care should be taken not to mix wools of different types unless, of course, you are making a multi-textured piece of woolwork.

The numbers on each chart are the Elizabeth Bradley wool numbers. As needleworkers tend to have their own favourite brands of wool I have given equivalent colour numbers on page 163 for several of the most popular and readily available makes. Most of the wool colours in our range are used somewhere in the book.

BUYING YARN

The colour of a wool may vary slightly between dye lots though the differences are minimal these days and will only very occasionally cause problems. For instance, a slight difference in the shade of a wool can result in a shadowy line across an area of background or a large section of the design. However, as carpet squares are divided by connecting lines of different colours and each piece in a set of chair seats is separated by space, it is not necessary to buy all the background wool that you might need for such a large project at once. Instead, you need only buy what will be used for each section.

STITCHES

The long history of the art of embroidery is interwoven with the story of man and the progress of civilizations through the centuries. Silk was already being woven in China in 3000 BC and it is known that fabrics were decorated with stitches in Egypt and the Far East as long ago as 2000 BC. The rich and exotic saga of stitchery has continued through the centuries right up to the present day although the actual techniques have changed very little. The same stitches were used by nuns in the fourteenth century as are employed by ladies of the Embroiderers Guild today.

Different periods and countries have tended to have their own name for each stitch and this makes it difficult to establish exactly how many varieties actually exist. Many of the names by which we identify them today are comparatively recent, for instance, Florentine stitch is also called Flame or Hungarian stitch, whereas in the seventeenth century it was known as Irish stitch. Tent stitch is one of the oldest and most commonly used, especially for covering large areas of canvas. It is sometimes

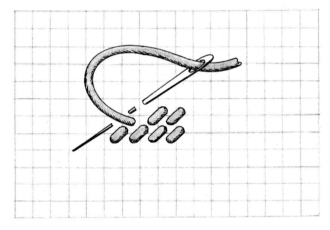

called half cross, needlepoint, or continental, stitch. When worked on fine canvas it is called petit point and when a larger version is used, it is known as gros point. Further confusion is caused by including all the pieces worked in half cross stitch under

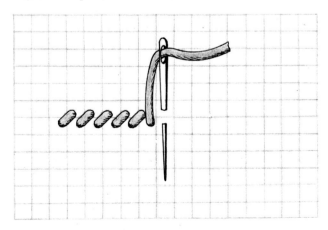

the general heading of 'tapestry'. Tapestry is in reality a woven fabric, and most of the 'tapestry' kits today are designed to be worked in tent stitch or half cross stitch.

Both of these variations on a basic half cross stitch look the same from the front of the work and are quick and easy to work. Ideally they should be worked on a canvas that is held taut in an embroidery frame. This is because all the stitches in the piece pull in one direction, from left to right, and the canvas can become distorted so that it ends up as a diamond or parellologram.

The use of another variation of tent stitch, called basketweave, can help to avoid mishapen finished pieces. It is worked from one corner of the canvas diagonally across to the other. Because the direction of the stitches at the back of the work changes with each row, the canvas is pulled both ways alternately

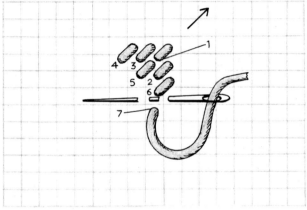

and ends up reasonably square. Basketweave also covers the canvas well and makes a slightly thicker piece of embroidery than either tent or half cross stitch. It can be very confusing to use for the detailed parts of a pattern and so often these are sewn in tent stitch while the background is completed in basketweave stitch.

Added thickness can be given to a background worked in simple tent stitch by a process known as tramming. A length of wool is laid down from one side of the canvas to the other before starting each row of stitches, which are then worked over the wool thread, totally hiding it. Tramming is most easily done on Penelope canvas. Sometimes it is possible to buy canvas with the central design already trammed in the different coloured wools.

(Far left) Tent stitch. Tent and half cross stitch are likely to distort the canvas as you work. Stretching the piece (see page 156) will be important once the needlework is complete.

(Left) Basketweave. The numbers are positioned to show the start of each stitch. The arrow shows the direction in which each stitch is made. Rows are worked alternately upwards and downwards along the diagonal.

(Bottom left) Half cross stitch. This is probably the most straightforward of stitches, but check that the canvas is being properly covered.

Cross stitch.

Pass the needle under one thread. Leave the knot on the surface – the thread can be stitched over later and the knot cut off.

Complete the stitch and then pass the needle under two threads.

Repeat the first step, passing the needle under one thread.

Once again, pass the needle under two threads.

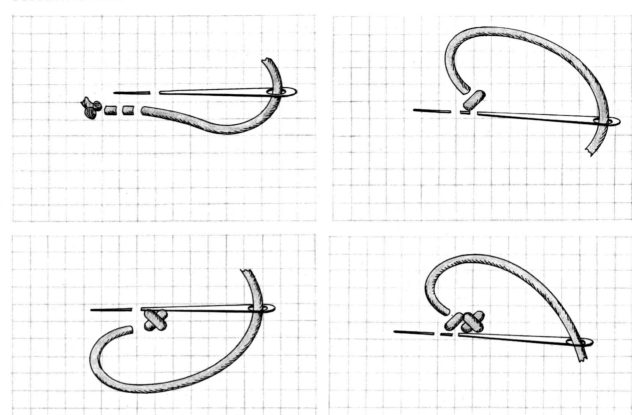

Each section of the pattern is then merely covered with the appropriate colour stitches.

My favourite stitch, and the one that I recommend be used for all the designs in this book, is cross stitch. It is an ancient stitch, as can be seen by its use on the vestments of early Coptic Christians. Cross stitch was used particularly extensively by the Victorians as they needed it to cover the newly invented Penelope canvas. Ten mesh was the most popular guage of this canvas in the nineteenth century and the soft German Berlin wool, so popular at that time, did not cover it adequately if tent or half cross stitch were used. The same is true to a certain extent with modern 10 mesh canvas and tapestry wool.

Cross stitch has several other advantages. One is that the finished pieces of needlework are thicker than those made with tent stitch and so they tend to be more hard wearing. As a stitch, it is easy to work and as each individual cross forms its own small square the pattern looks very distinct. The most important advantage of all, however, is that the canvas

does not become distorted as the work progresses. Each stitch pulls first to the right and then to the left and the piece remains square overall. A frame is therefore not necessary unless, of course, you prefer to work on one. The work can be held in the hand and rolled up as the work progresses. Working without a frame is also quicker because the stitch can be accomplished with the right or left hand working entirely on the front of the canvas. A frame holds the canvas taut which means that the needle needs to be pushed from back to front and *visa versa* to complete each stitch – a much slower process. Advocates for frames assure me that the quality of the finished work done on them is far superior to that done without them. Maybe they are right, but I do know that I cannot tell which of our finished pieces have been worked held in the hand or stretched on a frame – the quality seems to depend on the skill and experience of the needleworker.

As is the case with half cross stitch, there are a number of different methods of working complete cross stitch. The various techniques used in the past can be seen by studying the backs of original pieces of woolwork. The one illustrated opposite is that which I consider to be the best for working the charts in this book. The wool quantities that are given with each chart allow for the use of this type of cross stitch worked on 10 mesh interlock canvas. It is a very easy and satisfactory type of cross stitch, although somewhat extravagant with wool. Original pieces using it seem to have lasted particularly well, perhaps because the canvas is well covered and protected on both sides by the stitches. The finished pieces are certainly both hardwearing and satisfyingly square examples of needlework.

From the front, cross stitch looks like a close and even textured tent stitch and the work needs to be examined quite closely to see that each stitch is, in fact, a complete cross. If you pick up a square and feel the weight and thickness, the difference becomes clearer – it is far heavier and sturdier than a normal piece of needlepoint. Although these qual-

ities are an advantage if the piece is to be made into a cushion or a chair or stool seat, they are essential if it is destined to be part of a carpet. Squares worked in tent stitch would almost certainly need careful stretching and reshaping and however carefully this is done they always tend to creep back to a diamond shape – especially if they become damp.

The Victorians sometimes used stitches other than cross stitch and petit point to cover large areas of background. It made a change to be able to create a variety of interesting textures. Some of these stitches are mentioned in the chapter on patterned backgrounds and diagrams showing how they are worked are given below.

The finished appearance of a stitched piece of canvas depends on several factors. Generally, if the stitches are even, then the work will be smoother and look better. If the wool can be persuaded to pass through the canvas without jagging and twisting this makes an enormous difference. If wool is tugged and jerked then it tends to become matted and woolly

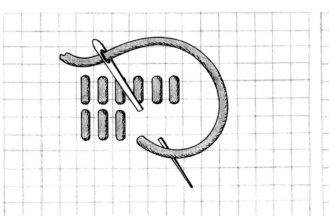

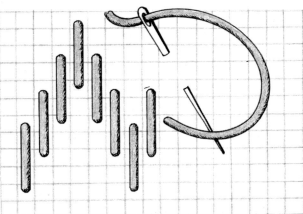

Gobelin stitch.

Florentine stitch.

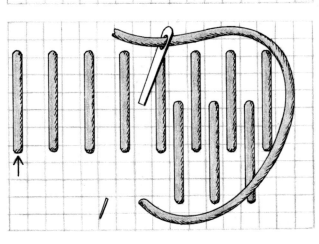

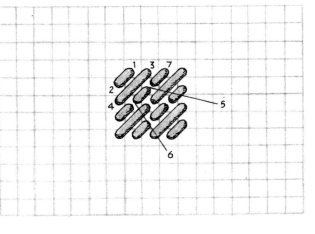

Brick stitch.

Mosaic stitch.

As with cross stitch, the starting point for any of these stitches is a matter of personal preference.

and loses its lustre. Practice and experience help but the length of each strand is also important. Not only do long lengths of wool twist more easily than short ones but they can also become thin and frayed. About 30 inches is a practical length. Another factor is the direction in which the wool is used: it has a right and a wrong way. If a length of wool is pulled between the fingers, one direction should feel smoother than the other. Always work with the wool passing through the canvas this smooth way and it will behave much better. If a length is being awkward, try turning it around.

TENSION

The term tension means how tight each stitch should be pulled. The quality of the finished piece can be affected by the tension of the stitches. They should not be pulled too tight or the wool becomes stretched and thin, nor should they be so loose as to form loops. The resulting work will be smoother and actually larger in area if the tension is kept reasonably loose. Tugging each stitch too tightly causes the canvas to become puckered and makes the whole piece slightly smaller in size. Ideally, the tension of each stitch should be the same throughout the piece and the ability to achieve this comes with practice as does an easy and personal rhythm of stitching.

UNPICKING STITCHES

It is easy, especially when tired, to make small mistakes when following a chart. Most of them can be put right quite easily by either undoing a few stitches and re-doing them, or by adapting that part of the pattern slightly so that your mistake just merges in with the rest of the pattern. No one is likely to examine every single stitch, and one could say that small variations add individuality. It is important, though, to get some details right, one stitch in the wrong place, in an eye for instance, could make quite a difference to the expression of a dog or cat.

If an area of stitches needs to be undone, this should be done with great care. First snip through each stitch with a small pointed pair of scissors: the cut ends can then be pulled out with the needle or a pair of tweezers. When the canvas is reworked, care should be taken to anchor down any stray ends of wool that are left with the new stitches. If a can-

vas thread does get cut by mistake when a stitch is being snipped, it is possible to repair it by cutting a small square of blank canvas from the side of the work, and tacking it behind the damaged area so that the position of the holes and the mesh coincide exactly. The new stitches can be worked through the main canvas and the patch and a practically invisible mend can be achieved.

WORKING FROM A CHART

Contrary to what many people think, working from a chart is very straight forward and once the eye has got used to following the squared pattern it can be followed quite easily. Each square on the chart represents one stitch but as each stitch is worked over a thread of canvas, it is the threads that should be counted, not the holes – hence the name counted thread work which is sometimes given to this sort of needlework.

Reading a chart becomes quite simple once this principle is established – all that is required is careful counting. Each square is coloured in a shade that is as similar as possible to the wool that will be used. As some of the colours are very close, symbols have been added where necessary for extra clarity.

The size of the finished piece of needlework made by following the chart will depend on the mesh size of the canvas used. In order to calculate how big the completed needlework will be, divide the number of squares on the chart by the mesh size of the canvas. For example; if a chart is 100 squares by 160 squares:

Mesh	Size of finished area of needlework
8 mesh canvas : $100/8 \times 160/8$ =	$12\frac{1}{2} \times 20$ inches (31.25 × 50cms)
10 mesh canvas : $100/10 \times 160/10$ =	10×16 inches (25 × 40cms)
12 mesh canvas : $100/12 \times 160/12$ =	$8\frac{1}{3} \times 13\frac{1}{3}$ inches (20.75 × 33.75cms)
20 mesh canvas : $100/20 \times 160/20$ =	5×8 inches (12.5 × 20cms)

Once the dimensions of the project are known, the canvas can be bought. A margin of about 3 inches (7.5cms) should be left all the way round.

Where you start to sew is, to a certain extent, a matter of preference, as is the way the design is worked. Some people start in the centre, work the

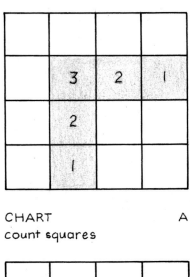

CHART   A
count squares

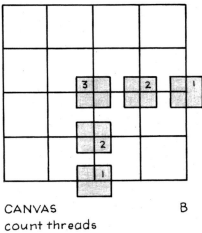

CANVAS   B
count threads

the right hand side. If there is a reasonable length of wool left in the needle at the end of the row, then use it to start the next row of stitches. If each background row is started with a new length of wool, each length will run out at approximately the same place creating a distinct and unattractive line on the front of the work. If, at the end of a row of background, you turn the canvas upside down you could work the next row back to where you started the previous one. This is much easier and saves a certain amount of starting and finishing off. Although it is quite common practice to do this, the evenness of the finished work is not as good because the background lines tend to separate out into pairs giving the work a slightly ridged appearance.

Most charts have small areas of a colour spread out over several different rows. Work from right to left as usual for each little row and start at the top (or bottom) of each patch of colour. Rather than working, say, three stitches, finishing off and then working another three above them, a small loop of wool can be left at the back of the canvas to connect the two tiny rows. These joining loops of wool should not be more than ½ inch (1.25cms) long or they will get caught up in the other stitches of the work and probably make it difficult to stretch properly should this be necessary. Sometimes a colour can be dotted about in small areas all over the chart. A stitch here, two there and so on. It is tempting to loop from one area to another but this is bad practice unless the dots are very close together.

As you become more experienced, you will no doubt develop your own favourite method of working the patterned area of a piece. The larger the areas of the colour on the chart, the quicker and easier it is to follow. It is the changing of the wool and the starting and finishing off that takes the time as much as the actual stitching. Many needleworkers are absolute perfectionists. They produce magnificent work in which each stitch exactly mirrors the equivalent square on the chart, the back of the work is often as exquiste as the front – most of us start out with this ideal in mind but fall down in the actual practice.

The group of needleworkers who are likely to have the most problems are those beginners who are absolute perfectionists. For them there is no pleasure in producing work that is not totally accurate and yet their lack of experience makes this difficult. I

When working from a chart each square represents one thread on the canvas.

picture first and then fill in the background later and this I believe is the correct procedure. Others – who are right handed – start at the top right hand corner and proceed downwards, this again is sensible as the worked area can be rolled up as the work proceeds, and stays clean (left-handed stitchers would begin in the top left hand corner). Personally, I like to start at the bottom right hand corner of the piece and work upwards because I like to see the pattern growing upwards from the bottom. Also, I find the stitch easier and quicker if worked in this direction. I tend to stitch the pictorial part of the design when I am feeling reasonably fresh and, if possible, when it is daylight; in the evening I can fill in the background while chatting or watching the television.

The background should be worked from right to left (or left to right – if you are left handed). Cut off the thread at the end of each row and start again on suggest that it would be sensible to start with the most simple patterns in this book and gradually proceed to the more complicated designs. There is a sense of achievement in finishing a piece of needlework that would be a pity to miss, and yet I meet many people who have sadly never completed their first attempt because of making a few mistakes early on.

STARTING AND FINISHING

Pieces of needlework that are obviously well executed tend to have very neat and tidy backs. To help achieve this, ends of wool should be cut off close to the work and long loops of wool stretching from one group of stitches to another should be avoided. If long ends and loops of more than ½ inch (1.25cm) are left, they become caught up with other stitches and the work can become terribly thick and matted.

Care should be taken to start and finish off each strand of wool properly. To begin stitching: a knot should be tied and then left on the front of the work about 1 inch (2.5cm) in front of where you intend to sew. Your stitches will hold the wool in place at the back and the knot can be snipped off when it is reached. To finish off: the length of wool should be taken to the back of the work and threaded through between six to ten stitches before being cut off. If only short ends of wool are interwoven at the start and finish, they can work loose very easily and necessitate constant repairs.

FITTING BORDERS

Some projects and their borders work out easily, others are a struggle. Rather than write reams of theoretical instructions the following charts illustrate the principles involved. Problems that arise and their solutions can be instructive in learning how to use not only these borders but also many others. The main queries are covered by showing first how to make a border for a cushion and second how to use the same border for the sides of a stool.

Don't forget that although the borders have been shown in one mixture of colours any combination can be tried. The colours on the sides of a stool should relate to those used in the design on the top and can be changed accordingly.

The Rose and Primula Border.
One repeat=40 stitches
Half a repeat=20 stitches
The depth=27 stitches

The ideal arrangement of the Rose and Primula Border around a centrepiece of 80 stitches square.

The ideal arrangement of the Rose and Primula Border around a centrepiece of 60 stitches square.

THE ROSE AND PRIMULA BORDER

This is a pretty flowered border which is useful for many purposes. It has a full repeat of (one rose AND one primula) 40 stitches and a half repeat (one rose OR one primula) of 20 stitches. The repeats are indicated on the chart on page 116.

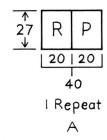

A

R = Rose
P = Primula

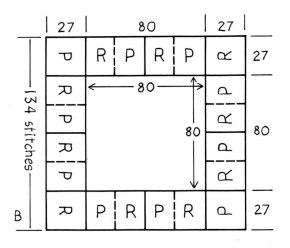

B

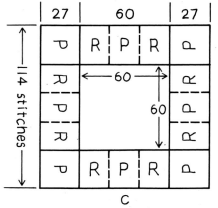

C

This is an attractive border for putting around a cushion piece, wallhanging or small rug. To make the chart easy to use, the dimensions of the centre-piece should ideally vary in units of at least 20 stitches or half a repeat. If the centrepiece doesn't and if it is at all possible, its size should be increased or reduced so that the rows of stitches are in multiples of 20.

If this is impossible, the pattern will have to be adapted and the best place to alter any design is at the free ends of a row of pattern. In this case, at the last rose or primula in that row. If the painted chart is studied carefully, it can be seen that a few simple, extra leaves and bits of stem have already been added to the flowers in each of the corners. These additions make the flowers and the space around them look more complete and deliberate.

To use this same border around the edge of a stool, box cushion or as a pelmet or tie-back involves similar but slightly different planning and layout. Again, if the length of the border can possibly be any multiple of 20 stitches it makes planning much easier.

The various factors involved when using this border can best be illustrated by planning a stool cover. In this case, the cover is to go on one of those rather attractive footstools shaped like a small square, flat box produced in large numbers early in the nineteenth century. They were usually fitted with flat bun feet each about 3 inches (7.5cms) in diameter. Smarter versions sported small feet resembling lion's paws made from brass. These box stools were almost invariably covered with needlework and make decorative little furnishing pieces. I am very fond of them and have had prototypes made with a top measuring 16×16 inches (40×40cms) and a drop of 5½ inches (13.75cms). Being simple in shape they are very easy to cover and make splendid needlework projects. A cover should be made in the traditional way in one piece with the edges tacked down underneath the stool, when it has been upholstered. The corners of the needlework are then sewn together using an invisible upholstery stitch. A square of hessian is tacked underneath the stool to make it look neat and tidy and lastly the bun feet are attached with large screws running up into the corner struts of the stool frame.

Many of the square pictorial charts in this book could be used to make an attractive top for such a stool and the various borders adapted to fit the sides.

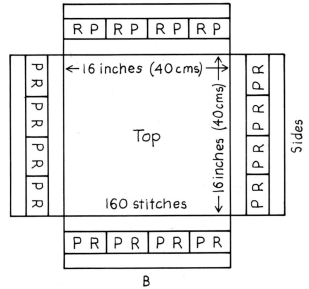

A typical Georgian box stool with bun feet.

The shape of the canvas and the arrangement of the Rose and Primula Border if making a cover for a box stool which is 16-inches (40-cms) square.

The Rose and Primula Border (page 116) works well and easily as a covering for the sides of this stool because it is a repeat of 40 stitches, or 4 inches (10cms), which fits exactly four times into the 16 inches (40cms), or 160 stitches, length of each side. However, the width of this border is only 2$\frac{7}{10}$ inches (6.8cms), or 27 stitches, while the drop of the stool is 5½ inches (13.75cms) or 55 stitches deep. A further 28 rows of stitches are needed to cover the full extent of the drop. This space could be filled in a number of ways. A second, identical, border could be sewn beneath the first, and the two divided by a single row of stitches in a contrasting colour. The second border could be placed directly beneath the first or it could be slightly displaced by half a repeat to add variety to the pattern on the side of the stool.

Alternatively, this additional 28 rows could be filled by an area of plain background or by various arrangements and widths of stripes. These should be worked in colours related to whatever design is to be used on the top of the stool.

Not all stool or cushion sides measure convenient multiples of 4 inches (10cms), however. Problems can arise if they are an awkward size such as 15½ inches (38.75cms). The first batch of stools that were made for me were slightly too small, their sides

Several examples of the way in which this border can be arranged around the sides of a stool. The border is indicated by the hatched areas.

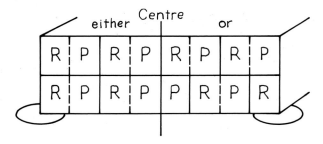

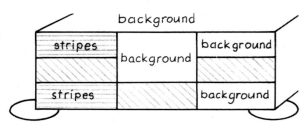

measure 15½ inches (38.75cms) or 155 stitches in length not the 16 inches (40cms) that was intended. Some adaption of the border pattern was therefore necessary for it to fit, since 155 is not a multiple of 20 or 40 stitches. As all four sides of a stool are the same length, only one side needs to be planned and it is best to think of each side as a rectangle measuring 15½ inches (38.75cms) by 5½ inches (13.75cms).

As any proposed arrangement of a border is much easier to plan with an even number rather than an odd number of stitches, it is worth adding one extra

A suggested arrangement for the border of a stool which is 15½-inches (38.75-cms) square. An extra stitch has been added to the top and sides to make each 156 stitches rather than 155 stitches long.

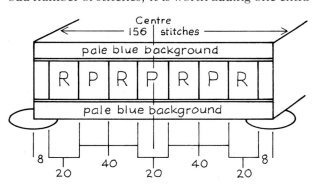

row on each of the sides to achieve this end. To match, make the square that forms the top of the stool measure 156 by 156 stitches rather than 155. This slight increase in size will not make any difference to the fit of the cover. Start planning the sides at their centre and work outwards. Centre one of the half repeats, say the primula, and then work towards the ends. In this way, you would arrive at 7 half repeats in all (140 stitches). Divide the remaining 16 stitches into two, leaving 8 at each end, as in the diagram. This organization of the Rose and Primula border is just one of the possible arrangements which could be worked out and then repeated on all four sides. The pattern looks attractive, considered and deliberate. The rose at the end of each strip could be finished off with some extra leaves to fill up the space.

THE TASSEL BORDER

This border features a row of tassels that hang from a web-like tracery of threads so that the pattern rather resembles a length of a tasselled lampshade braid (see chart on page 121). It is a most attractive, simple and yet decorative edging with a repeat of 10 stitches. It also serves to illustrate a second method of turning a corner. The only problem is that, as it stands, it just will not go round a right angle easily. I tried numerous combinations and permutations and each arrangement ended up more complicated and unattractive than the last. Eventually I resorted to the ruse of joining each length of tassels with a corner motif, in this case a rosette set in a small square of needlework (see chart on page 121). The inspiration came from some rather elegant picture frames that were popular at the end of the eighteenth century. Their sides are made of reeded, pine mouldings painted black and each corner features a gilt rosette mounted on the middle of a plain black square. I feel that my four needlework rosettes are just as effective. The border is both smart and adaptable in this form. As the repeat is a mere 10 stitches it should be reasonably easy to adapt any centrepiece you choose to work to fit into a frame of this border. Just add or subtract a few rows from round the central piece until it measures any multiple of 10 stitches.

The tasseled edging can be used to make very decorative pelmets, as well as elegant sides for stools or box cushions. The square stool can once more be used to illustrate the various points that might arise in covering such items. Again, the edging is rather too narrow for the 5½-inch (13.75-cm) drop of the little stools. However, this difficulty is soon overcome as the tassels can be elongated by up to an inch (2.5cms) or more without appearing ridiculous. An area of plain background or a stripe or two can be worked at the bottom to fill the remaining space. As before, the border fits on to the sides of the 16-inch (40-cm) version of the stool perfectly since 16

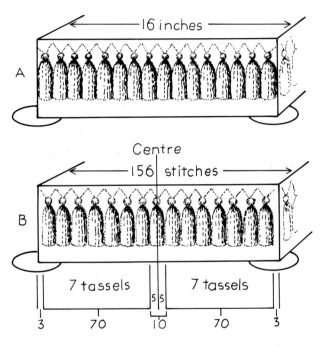

inches (40cms), or 160 stitches (on 10 mesh canvas), is easily divisible by the basic repeat of 10 stitches.

Again, however, some forward planning is needed to make it fit a more awkward size such as the 15½-inch (38.75-cm) stool and once more it would be easier to work out if the top square and each side measured 156 stitches rather than 155 stitches.

The diagram shows the border adapted to fit this length. A tassel should be placed in the centre of each side and the others worked out from it in both directions. Three rows of stitches will be left over at each end. These can be worked with only the tracery part of the design, omitting the tassel. Again, all four sides should be worked in the same way.

THE IVY BORDER

This border (for chart, see page 120) has a long repeat of 92 stitches and the design is complicated by lots of little tendrils waving about making it difficult to manoeuvre round corners. It can be done, but not in an exact manner. To make it easier to work out, I use several photocopies of the chart which I cut up and fiddle about with until the pieces make acceptable joins at all four corners. As long as none of the main blue green leaves are cut in half the border looks fine. A little improvisation is needed to organize the tendrils, however.

JOINING PIECES OF CANVAS TOGETHER

It is very useful to be able to join pieces of canvas together without the join showing on the right side of the work. Often needlework kits are designed for making a square cushion or a piece of some pre-destined shape or size. The stool or chair you may wish to cover could be oblong, hexagonal or just bigger than the kit. In such cases it is useful to be able to add on extra sections of canvas so that pieces can be made the right shape and size. It is important to make sure that exactly the same mesh and type of canvas are used to extend the main piece and that the direction of the canvas runs the same way.

Two pieces of canvas are joined together by overlapping their edges and then sewing through the double layer. The threads and holes must be lined up so that they coincide exactly and then tacked in position. A T-shaped tack worked in wool works well to stop them sliding out of place. The wider the overlap, the stronger the join. At least four rows of cross stitch are necessary to join carpet squares together. The patchwork cushion on page 141 is connected by three rows, one green and two yellow ochre. It is a smaller piece and so fewer are needed. However many rows of stitches are used, the principle is the same.

Where two pieces are to be joined, leave the underneath one untrimmed. If, as an example, four joining rows are used, trim the canvas of the top piece back to the fourth thread. Cut as near as possible to thread five so that little ends of cut canvas are left sticking out, these ends will help to prevent thread four from unravelling. Work rows one to

An arrangement of the Tassel Border on a 16-inch (40-cm) stool. As the design is based on a 10-stitch repeat, it fits exactly.

However, for a 15½-inch (38.75-cm) stool, the arrangement needs more careful planning.

three through both layers of canvas. As row four is worked, the little ends of canvas that were left sticking out can be cut off close to the thread as you come to them along the row.

Where four squares or pieces join, the stitching will be through four layers of canvas. Tack this section in place very carefully and be very gentle with the canvas at the central point – if the canvas unravels it is more difficult to achieve a perfect join. The canvas left sticking out at the back can be trimmed up to the stitching line leaving a practically invisible join at both back and front. It does take practice to make a perfect join but with perseverance it becomes easier.

MAKING UP CARPETS

Victorian carpets were often constructed from separate squares of woolwork which were joined together and then edged with a border. The individual sections were generally small enough to be manageable and were easily transportable. A large carpet made from a single piece of canvas would be awkward and heavy to handle while being made – indeed, one would probably need a suitcase rather than a workbag to carry it around. An infinite variety of shapes and sizes of rugs can be constructed in this way, each made with a different number of squares of various designs and a border. Every example can be an individual and totally unique piece.

Making and joining a carpet is not difficult but it does need a certain amount of forward planning. First, decide what sort of size and shape rug you would like to make, which border you want to use and how many central squares you are prepared to sew and then plan from there. All the stitches in

the completed piece should run in the same direction. Secondly, to fit together easily, all the pieces in a carpet must be made with the correct number of stitches. Check and count very carefully as the various sections are made up. It is easier to change the number of stitches in the central section rather than in the border which will have a predetermined repeat which probably cannot be altered easily. Note that the number of rows in the central section must be a multiple of 10 or 20 rows if the Rose and Primula Border (page 116) is being used; and a multiple of 10 for the Tassel Border (page 121) if they are to fit without alteration.

When planning a carpet, bear in mind that any joins in the lengths of border should line up half way down the side of a central square rather than where two squares join. This will ensure maximum

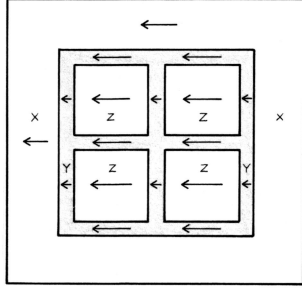

The layout of any carpet which has been made with a number of central squares. Note that the stitches have all been worked in the same direction.

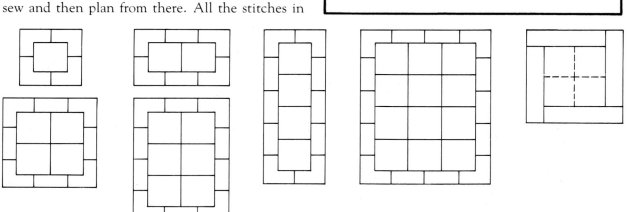

Several examples of the ways in which carpet piece can be joined together.

strength in the completed piece. If a join were to run right from one side of the carpet to the other it could prove to be a point of weakness.

The joining rows generally look better worked in a contrasting colour. It is difficult to join canvas totally invisibly and a band of a different wool framing each square is both practical and traditional. Remember to allow for these rows in your carpet plan. The band can be of any width but it should be at least four rows wide for it to have sufficient strength.

The carpet should also be finished off with a neat outside edge. Trim the unworked canvas all around the edge to about eight rows, fold it over and stitch over the fold. The stitches can be either worked in wool of the same shade as the outermost row or in a contrasting colour. First stitch one way all the way round, and then back in the other direction.

If the carpet is to be laid on a wooden or stone floor it is advisable to line it. Upholstery hessian makes a good backing fabric and to stop it bagging, it should be attached to the back of the carpet with rows of tacking stitches, each just catching the back of the piece lightly. This is best done with the carpet laid flat on the floor or face down on a table. Trim the edges of the hessian, fold them under, and sew the folded edge to the inside of the last binding row of stitches. If a carpet is to be laid on to a fitted carpet it is best left unlined – it will slip around less. Just hem stitch cotton tape or upholstery webbing along the inside edge of the carpet all the way round the outside. The same tape can be sewn over all the joints to give added strength if this is desired. If pressing is necessary, it should be done on the back of the piece with a steam iron.

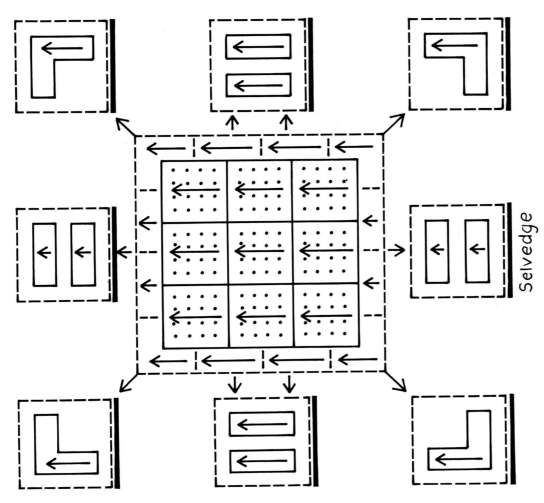

This diagram shows the direction of stitching on the various sections which may make up a carpet.

TREATMENT OF COMPLETED PIECES

STRETCHING

If a piece of needlework has become distorted, it must be stretched back into shape before being used. If cross stitch has been used then it should already be square, but if not, then the piece may be distorted into a diamond shape and will need to be blocked. This is done by spraying the back with water so that the piece is wet but not soaking. Then stretch the piece by placing it face down on a sheet of blockboard and pulling it into shape. Quite firm but careful tugging will probably be necessary before the canvas is restored to its original shape and size. The stretched needlework can be held in place by carpet tacks or drawing pins around the edge of the canvas. Leave it pinned out until it is perfectly dry. It can be left for several days if necessary. Pieces that have been worked in half cross stitch rather than cross stitch may then need to be fixed in their new, 'perfect', shape or they will tend to creep back into being diamonds. A covering of wallpaper paste spread on the back of the pinned out piece and then left to dry should help.

Some people spray the back of a finished piece with spray starch to fix any loose ends of wool in place.

CLEANING WOOLWORK PIECES

For the purposes of cleaning it is helpful to regard woolwork as a thick upholstery fabric. It can be washed if absolutely necessary using a gentle soap powder and warm water but it is better to have pieces of work dry cleaned, especially if they have already been made up into cushions. The colours of modern tapestry wool are fast and do not run but washing softens the threads of the canvas and the piece can become puckered if the woolwork and its backing shrink to different degrees.

If the piece of woolwork has been used to cover a stool or chair then dry cleaning is impossible. If this is the case, vacuum clean the surface to remove any dust or loose dirt particles and then sponge with an upholstery foam. Wool is protected from dirt to a certain extent by its own natural oils but extra protection can be given by spraying a freshly completed piece with Scotch Guard.

Antique woolwork should never be washed by an amateur. Many of the colours run and the canvas fibres will have been weakened by age. Water would soften these fibres and might cause them to disintegrate. If serious cleaning is necessary then it is a job for a professional textile restorer.

UPHOLSTERED FURNITURE

Pieces of woolwork make excellent covers for most types of upholstered furniture. Stools and dining chairs are the usual items covered but in the past sofas, armchairs and ottomans were all popular subjects. Antique upholstered furniture can still be brought relatively cheaply.

Before the new needlework cover is attached, it is advisable to have the item of furniture upholstered, or at least rewebbed and covered with calico if this is necessary. It is well worth having this done professionally by traditional methods – after all it takes many hours to make a needlework cover and it would be a pity to tack it onto a piece of furniture that will need restoration or repair before very long. Canvas worked in cross stitch can be quite heavy if it is a large piece. It will need to be well stretched as it is tacked down to the frame of the chair or stool, and again it is worth having this done by an upholsterer who has the correct tools and knows where and how to cut the canvas most effectively. Alternatively, many educational authorities offer evening classes in upholstery.

Many classic pieces of furniture are now reproduced and the manufacturers or stockists should be able to provide you with the templates for the covers of such pieces. Otherwise, the best way to determine the shape and size of a chair or stool cover is to remove the original cover and use it as a pattern. If this is not possible, measure the dimensions of the seat and draw the shape on the canvas leaving a margin of at least 3ins (7.5cms) all the way round.

CUSHIONS

The majority of woolwork pieces sewn today are made into cushions. After spending many hours sewing a cushion piece it is a shame not to make it up in the best way possible and have a really handsome piece that will last for many years. Velvet or silk was the most usual backing material for Victorian cushions, or occasionally ottoman cloth or a fine woven worsted wool resembling flannel was used as an alternative. All these fabrics work well. The material should be reasonably thick and of as good quality as you can manage so that it will wear well. Cotton upholstery velvet looks better than draylon and a thick moiré silk makes a splendid backing fabric. Thin silk is attractive but it tends to pucker when sewn on to the relatively thick worked canvas: if you wish to use this sort of silk it is best to give it more body with some sort of stiffening. Various iron-on products are available and work well for this purpose.

Zips are a relatively modern invention and before their arrival cushions were made up with a gap left at the bottom, which was stitched up after the cushion pad had been inserted. A zip allows the pad to be removed easily, it is best sewn in at the bottom of the piece where it will not show.

Many Victorian cushions were embellished with a cord sewn round the edge and a tassel at each corner. A vast range of exquisite silk and woollen trimmings were available in the nineteenth century, many of them made by hand. Good modern versions are hard to find and many of them are made from acrylic fibres which are really too shiny and bright in colour to be used with woolwork. However, a well chosen cord and tassel finishes off any cushion beautifully.

Cord unravels very quickly if the ends are left free so they should be bound with thread or a small piece of Scotch tape at all times. The cord should be attached to the cushion by hand, stitching it all the way round using button thread and a curved needle. The cord must not be pulled tight: as it is sewn on, it should lie easy and unstretched against the edges of the cushion. It is best to start at the bottom of the piece, at the end of the zip or gap left for inserting the feather pad. Poke one end of the cord into the gap in the seam and sew it in place. Continue sewing round back to the starting point. The far end of the cord should then be pushed in next to the first and the two firmly stitched in place together to make as invisible a joint as possible. The tassels can be added as each corner is reached. Each tassel has a loop on top and the cord should be pushed through this loop to attach the tassel.

Piping, made from silk cut on the cross and wrapped around piping cord, can be used as an alternative trim. A small piece of needlework can be extended by using it as the centre piece of a fabric frame made from strips of material with their corners mitred.

TIE-BACKS AND PELMETS

The Rose Swag chart on page 56 is the perfect design to use if you wish to make curtain tie-backs or pelmets. For tie-backs, further background should be added to the basic chart as outlined here. If the curtains you wish to keep back are thicker than average

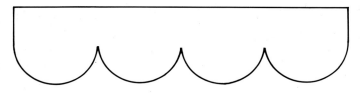

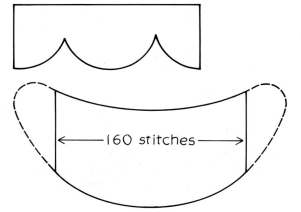

Two arrangements of the Rose Swag to make pelmets to fit different size windows.

A tie-back opened out to show its basic outline, and a tie-back in place folded around a curtain.

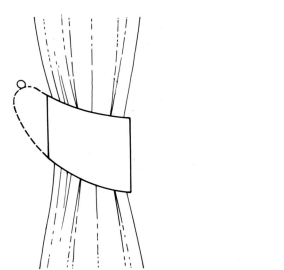

it would be advisable to make the tie-backs bigger. To do this, add extra rows of stitches all the way around making sure the basic outline is maintained.

FRAMING

Pictures made from pieces of woolwork were very popular in the nineteenth century. Many of these pictures have since been made into cushions though some of the larger examples have survived in their original form often in elaborately carved rococo or gilded frames. Overall, however, the most popular form of frame moulding throughout the last century was made of pine covered with a thin maple veneer. The tawny spotted wood complemented the brightly coloured woolwork pieces perfectly. Modern maple frames are very similar to nineteenth-century examples.

Victorian houses were heated by means of coal or wood fires. Upholstery, curtains and pictures tended to become discoloured by the smoke and fumes and so generally framed pieces of woolwork were placed behind glass. This protected them not only from the smoke, but also from damage caused by moths. However, it is interesting to note that most of the cushions, chair covers and carpets that were made from Berlin woolwork in the nineteenth century seem to have survived looking remarkably fresh and clean even after a hundred years of wear and pollution. Maybe glazing was not strictly necessary after all, perhaps the oil in the wool provides a certain amount of protection on its own, repelling the dirt and tar. Woolwork certainly looks more attractive unglazed as the glass tends to reflect the light, dim the colours and squash the stitches unless a gilt frame liner is used.

Before framing, it is essential to stretch the piece. Traditionally, the work was tacked to a specially made wooden stretcher before being placed in the frame. However, stretching the work over a 16-inch (40-cm) square piece of hardwood works nearly as well. The hardboard should be slightly smaller than the frame. Place the needlework face downwards on a table, spray lightly with water and lay the hardboard on top. Using a thin string or strong twine lace the top and the bottom together gradually pulling it tight as you go. This should be done gently because if the canvas is suddenly jerked tight it can tear: it needs time to stretch to its fullest extent. When you feel that it is sufficiently tight, the process can be repeated with the lacing running from one side to the other. When all the strings are taut the corners can be stitched down and the stretched piece placed in the frame. The picture should be backed with a piece of card or mounting board cut to the correct shape. This is then fastened in place with panel pins or a framing gun and the join between card and frame covered with a strip of gummed brown paper tape. I think that it is a good custom to write your name and the date on the back of a framed woolwork. It adds interest and is a useful record. Your descendants or antique dealers of the future will be most grateful that the piece has been dated for them.

ELIZABETH BRADLEY NEEDLEWORK KITS

The following designs in this book are available in full kit form from any of the Elizabeth Bradley distributors as well as leading stores and needlework shops:

			Page
A Wreath of Roses	16.0×16.0 ins (40×40 cms)	Black/Cream	48
Repeating Roses	16.0×16.0 ins (40×40 cms)	Black/Cream	103
Violets	16.0×16.0 ins (40×40 cms)	Black/Cream	64
Patchwork Pieces	16.0×16.0 ins (40×40 cms)	Black/Cream	133–40

Each kit contains:
* Canvas (10 to the inch interlock) printed with the design in colour.
* A full size coloured chart to help work the design accurately.
* Sufficient wool to work the design in a full cross stitch.
* Comprehensive instructions and a history leaflet.
* Background wool and a background wool changing leaflet.
* A woolcard with samples of all the colours used in the design.
* Two needles.
* All these components are enclosed in an attractive box which make the kits suitable as gift items.

To work any of the designs from the charts in this book, the following materials are available from Elizabeth Bradley Designs and their distributors (see pages 161-2):
* Wool in any of the standard Elizabeth Bradley colours, wound onto cards (10 yards and 30 yards).
* 10 mesh interlock canvas, 1 metre wide, available by the metre (minimum length 1 metre).

In addition, the following standard designs are available in full kit form from any of the Elizabeth Bradley distributors and leading stores and needlework shops:

THE VICTORIAN ANIMAL SERIES
1) The Cream Cat
2) The Spaniel
3) The Cockerel
4) The Mother Hen
5) The Parrot
6) The Three Birds
7) Toby The Pug
8) The Contented Cat
9) The Spotted Dog
10) The Squirrel
11) The Lion
12) The Elephant

THE FOUR SEASONS VICTORIAN FLOWER SERIES
13) Spring
14) Summer
15) Autumn
16) Winter

THE FRUITS OF THE EARTH SERIES
17) Strawberries
18) A Bowl of Fruit
19) Vegetables
20) A Wreath of Herbs

Kits 1 to 20 all measure 16×16 ins (40×40 cms). They can be used to make cushions, pictures and stool covers or joined together to make needlework carpets.
A Flowered Bell Pull (Kit – BP) can also be used as a carpet border around any four squares.
A Ribbon and Bow Border Kit can be used to edge carpets of various sizes (Kits A, B and C).

THE BEASTS OF THE FIELD SERIES
These four designs feature portraits of naïve farm animals and each measures 13×20 ins (32.5× 50 cms).
21) The Gloucester Old Spot Sow with her Piglets 23) The Suffolk Punch with a Hound
22) The Shorthorn Ox   24) Two Fat Suffolk Lambs

The following items and services can also be obtained from the distributors listed below.
* Cord, tassels and brass bell pull ends.
* A cushion-making service.
* A framing service.
* An illustrated 28 page colour brochure.
* Worked examples of all the designs shown in this book.
* A Woolfax containing samples of the full range of Elizabeth Bradley wools.

ELIZABETH BRADLEY DISTRIBUTORS

Australia

Lauren Exclusives
53 William Edward Street
Longueville
New South Wales 2066
Australia

Tel: (2) 427 51 47
Fax: (2) 602 87 41

British Isles

Elizabeth Bradley Designs Ltd.
1 West End
Beaumaris
Anglesey
N Wales
LL58 8BD

Tel: (0248) 811055
Fax: (0248) 811118

Denmark

Sommerfuglen
Holbergsgade 19
1057 Copenhagen K
Denmark

Tel: (33) 32 82 90

France

Voisine
12 Rue De L'Eglise
92200 Neuilly Sur Seine
Paris
France

Tel: (1) 46 37 54 60

Germany

Offerta Plaumann
Odenwaldstraße 5
D–6080
Groß-Gerau
W Germany

Tel: (61) 52 56 964
Fax: (61) 52 53 705

Holland

Meander
Industrieweg 7
2254 AE Voorschoten
Holland

Tel: (01717) 7642
Fax: (01717) 9741

A large carpet featuring Elizabeth Bradley designs – twelve animals and a border design. From top left to bottom right, the designs are:

Row 1: The Cockerel, The Three Birds, The Cream Cat. Row 2: The Spaniel, The Squirrel, The Elephant. Row 3: The Lion, The Parrot (see chart on page 24), The Spotted Dog. Row 4: Toby The Pug, The Contented Cat, The Mother Hen.

The border is a Ribbon and Bow Border.

Italy

Sybilla
Via Rizzoli 7
40125 Bologna
Italy

Tel: (51) 75 88 44
Fax: (51) 657 01 70

Spain

Ana Cardenal De Dolz
Juan Bravo 26
28006 Madrid
Spain

Tel: (1) 435 47 76
Fax: (1) 571 32 72

United States of America

Elizabeth Bradley Inc.
P O Box 525
Lisle
Illinois 60532
U.S.A.

Tel: (708) 964 7444
Fax: (708) 983 3290

USEFUL ADDRESSES – MANUFACTURERS AND SUPPLIERS

The following companies supply upholstered furniture suitable for covering with needlework.

Alison Stewart
Hart Villa Interiors
Sheep Street
Stow on the Wold
Cheltenham
Glos. GL54 1AA

Tel: (0451) 30392

George Smith
587–589 Kings Road
London SW6 2EH

Tel: (071) 384 1004

67–73 Spring Street
New York
NY10012 U.S.A.

Tel: (212) 226 4747

Rupert Hanbury Antiques (Stools)
The Kennels
Bartlow
Cambridge CB1 6PW

Tel: (0223) 893535

Upholstery Trimmings

Distinctive Trimmings
17 Kensington Church Street
London W8 4LF

Tel: (071) 937 6174

Making up Woolwork Slippers

Trickers
67 Jermyn Street
London SW1 6MY

Tel: (071) 930 6395

Pure Silk Thread

Mulberry Silks
Unit 12a
Worcester Industrial Estate
Worcester Road
Chipping Norton
Oxon OX7 5XW

Tel: (0608) 644119

CONVERSION CHARTS

WOOL NUMBERS – EQUIVALENT COLOURS
Number in brackets = nearest available equivalent colour

Elizabeth Bradley	Paternayan	Anchor	DMC	Appleton	Elizabeth Bradley	Paternayan	Anchor	DMC	Appleton
A1	924	(3290)	7221	141	D7	(710)	0735	7785	844
A2	923	(0498)	7950	221	D8	(752)	0563	7676	312
A3	(933)	3098	7194	222	D9	751	3013	7485	313
A4	(932)	3008	7354	223	D10	750	0720	7487	314
A5	931	(3166)	7196	224	D11	(750)	0845	7490	315
A6	930	(3152)	7147	226					
A7	920	0341	7449	127	E1	(444)	0902	7724	761
A8	900	0897	7219	759	E2	443	3190	7423	901
A9	(485)	0377	7465	122	E3	(435)	0623	(7455)	763
A10	404	0369	(7465)	302	E4	442	3064	7494	902
A11	922	0745	7632	125	E5	441	(3065)	7421	903
					E6	495	0501	7846	697
B1	494	0421	7451	702	E7	(740)	0723	7497	904
B2	(406)	3241	7162	202	E8	(720)	(0348)	7457	766
B3	486	0744	7144	203	E9	412	0650	(7845)	767
B4	485	0914	7166	204	E10	(412)	(0724)	7499	905
B5	873	0741	7124	205	E11	411	(0351)	7479	304
B6	872	0339	7356	206	E12	410	(0358)	7459	305
B7	860	3025	7178	207					
B8	870	0340	7447	208	F1	261	0402	BLANC	991
B9	831	(0700)	7920	865	F2	262	(0402)	BLANC	992
B10	851	0412	(7184)	866	F3	263	0386	ECRU	882
B11	840	0019	7127	504	F4	465	3202	7500	988
					F5	455	(0441)	7491	984
C1	645	0388	7492	691	F6	(644)	(0388)	7523	951
C2	744	0721	7523	692	F7	(443)	3190	7524	952
C3	742	3230	(7472)	693	F8	(442)	3045	7525	953
C4	733	0727	(7473)	473	F9	(441)	0418	7514	914
C5	732	0734	7782	695	F10	(452)	0419	7490	955
C6	731	3002	7781	696	F11	(451)	0420	7488	916
C7	723	0728	7767	475					
C8	722	0325	7444	476	G1	455	0391	7452	981
C9	884	0835	7175	861	G2	454	3057	7520	982
C10	(881)	0427	7176	863	G3	453	0713	7519	183
C11	880	0428	7446	479	G4	(424)	0714	7413	986
					G5	424	3041	7518	184
D1	755	3370	7905	841	G6	432	0905	(7499)	186
D2	743	(3285)	7493	331	G7	431	0986	7938	187
D3	727	3229	7503	471	G8	(422)	0420	7489	582
D4	(712)	(3230)	(7504)	842	G9	450	0360	7515	584
D5	(753)	0565	7473	843	G10	459	0987	7419	588
D6	(751)	0308	7677	311	G11	220	0403	NOIR	993

Elizabeth Bradley	Paternayan	Anchor	DMC	Appleton
H1	(464)	0390	7390	971
H2	(202)	3363	7331	972
H3	(453)	(0438)	7415	973
H4	(452)	(0438)	7416	974
H5	451	(0985)	7529	976
H6	204	3202	7270	989
H7	203	0397	7282	962
H8	202	(0397)	7618	963
H9	(202)	0398	(7273)	964
H10	201	0399	7620	965
H11	200	0400	7622	967
I1	694	0280	7361	252
I2	653	0647	(7361)	241
I3	644	0842	(7493)	332
I4	652	0962	7363	242
I5	643	3087	7373	343
I6	(652)	(3087)	7362	344
I7	(643)	0647	(7362)	345
I8	642	0843	(7355)	334
I9	651	3101	(7582)	244
I10	641	0424	7391	336
I11	640	0715	7425	348
J1	605	0858	7400	351
J2	(604)	0213	7402	352
J3	(613)	(0240)	7382	353
J4	(613)	0242	7424	354
J5	603	0215	7384	355
J6	(692)	0638	7364	255
J7	691	0268	7547	546
J8	690	0626	7367	357
J9	(600)	0269	7379	548
J10	693	0733	7770	544
J11	692	3236	7988	545
K1	203	0504	7928	151
K2	202	0440	7321	291
K3	604	0859	7870	292
K4	603	0860	7392	293
K5	602	0861	7404	294
K6	(600)	0862	7396	297
K7	(660)	0625	7398	298
K8	524	0837	7322	641
K9	534	0505	7335	642
K10	662	(0506)	7702	644

Elizabeth Bradley	Paternayan	Anchor	DMC	Appleton
K11	(660)	0712	7408	647
L1	506	0738	7322	521
L2	514	3195	7692	152
L3	534	0505	7323	154
L4	533	3197	7327	155
L5	532	3050	7326	156
L6	531	0507	7701	158
L7	530	0615	7429	159
L8	(534)	(0504)	7292	921
L9	(513)	0704	7293	922
L10	512	0432	7592	324
L11	510	0850	7297	928
M1	(583)	(0162)	(7926)	565
M2	502	0613	7650	566
M3	501	0706	7306	853
M4	515	0144	7715	876
M5	(564)	0431	(7715)	886
M6	563	(0118)	(7799)	741
M7	(563)	0160	7799	742
M8	570	0601	7308	852
M9	572	0851	7299	929
M10	(312)	0620	7243	105
M11	(320)	0125	(7245)	106
N1	(473)	(0636)	7232	931
N2	(922)	(0983)	7234	932
N3	(921)	(3053)	7236	933
N4	(920)	0873	7238	934
N5	(914)	0604	7213	711
N6	(913)	0869	7223	712
N7	(912)	0870	7226	713
N8	(910)	0605	(7167)	715
N9	323	0502	(7262)	603
N10	(312)	0872	(7266)	605
N11	(311)	0652	(7268)	606

LENGTHS OF DIFFERENT MANUFACTURERS' SKEINS AND HANKS

	Skein	Hank
Elizabeth Bradley (on cards)	10yd (9.2m)	30yd (27.6m)
Paternayan	8yd (7.3m)	40yd (36.9m)
Anchor	10.8yd (10m)	–
DMC	8.8yd (8m)	–
Appleton	10yd (9.2m)	60yd (55m)

ACKNOWLEDGMENTS

My grateful thanks to the following:

Miss Bette Anderson, Mrs Lavinia Chapman, Mrs Joan Eyles, Mrs Mary Hamlyn, David Lord Lawrence, The Countess of Lisburn and Mrs Pamela Quail – who were all kind enough to let me borrow original Berlin Woolwork charts or to send me photographs of Victorian pieces in their possession.

All the needlewomen and men who stitched the prototypes for this book with such skill and patience. Mrs Jan Bieniek, Mrs Carciero, Mr R and Olwen Chapple, Tarcie Connor, Mrs Anthea Davies, Mrs Jill Evans, Mrs Jenny Gleave, Mrs Sharon Granton, Mrs Jane Handy, Mrs Mary Hill, Mrs Anwen Hughes, Mrs Awena Jones, Mrs Gillian Jones, Mr Gerrie Kostick, Mrs Lynn Page, Mrs S L Peters, Mrs Joan Price, Mrs Heulwen Renshaw, Mrs Bethan Rowlands, Mrs Nia Rowlands, Mrs Denise Sheridan, Miss Jenny Strom, Mrs Mairwen Strom, Mr & Mrs Gordon Tucker, Mrs Ann Turnbull, Mrs Maureen Underwood, Miss Sheena Walker, Mr Maurice Wells, Mrs Betty Lloyd Williams, Miss Rosemary Williams, Mrs Margaret Woods.

Linda Gumb who lent me so many superb pieces of Victorian Woolwork from her lovely shop. She can be found at: Linda Gumb, 9 Camden Passage, London N1 (Tel: 071-354 1184).

My parents, Jack and Rosemary Rendall, and Victoria Gruffudd Jones who supplied not only a vast array of props but also much valuable advice.

Mr A Jackson who upholstered all the pieces in this book. His premises are at: Unit 15, Penrhosgarnedd Industrial Estate, Llangefni, Anglesey, Gwynedd, North Wales, LL77 7JA (Tel: 0248 724905).

The publishers also wish to thank the following:

Paula Pryke Flowers, Penton Street, London N1 who supplied all the flowers, loaned pot plants and dried flowers and made the twiggy frame on page 27; Crocodile Antiques, 257 Archway Road, London N6 who lent the black cast-iron fireplace on page 44 and the firetools on page 31; Valerie Wade, 108 Fulham Road, London SW6 who lent the large Papier mâché tray on page 44; 'Collectables', 18 The Mall, Camden Passage, London N1 who lent the small metal tray on page 107; The Gallery of Antique Costume and Textiles, 2 Church Street, London NW8 who lent the purple crushed velvet, the damask curtains and the tassels on page 63; Danielle Hartwright at Liberty, London W1 who lent the Victorian Needlework sofa on page 22; Town and Country Conservatories, 8 & 9 Murray Street, London N1 who lent the Winterthur Garden Bench on page 19; The Victorian Door Shop, 484 Hornsey Road, London N19 who lent the French Windows on page 58.

INDEX